GANGLAND

A GLOBAL HISTORY OF GANG WAR, GANGSTERS AND CRIMINAL CULTURE

MICHAEL JOHNSTONE

Capella

This edition printed in 2004 for
Bookmart Limited
Registered Number 2372865
Trading as Bookmart Limited
Blaby Road, Wigston,
Leicester LE18 4SE

©2004 Arcturus Publishing Limited
26/27 Bickels Yard, 151-153 Bermondsey Street
London SE1 3HA

British Library Cataloguing-in-Publication Data: a catalogue
record for this book is available from the British Library

ISBN 1-84193-214-0

Edited by Paul Whittle

Jacket design by Alex Ingr
Typeset by Mike Harrington, MATS

Printed in China

CONTENTS

INTRODUCTION

*Members of the Clanton Gang (left to right Tom McLaury, Frank McLaury and Billy Clanton)
shot by Wyatt Earp during the famous 'Gunfight at the OK Corral', Tombstone, Arizona, 26 October 1881.*

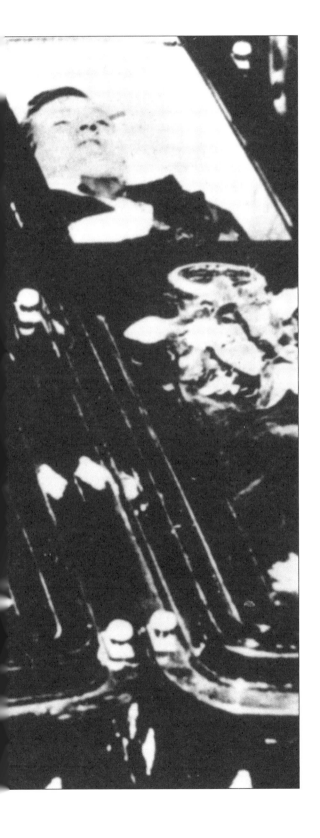

BELONGING to a gang can be a (comparatively) innocent childhood pleasure. William Brown, Richmal Crompton's young hero, for example, was the leader of such a group – The Outlaws – which 'met secretly every half-holiday in a disused barn about a quarter of a mile from William's house'. In their daydreams they were pirates, robbers, kidnappers and master criminals.

Oh, the innocent joys of childhood.

There was nothing innocent about the 'Gang of Four' – Zhang Chunquiao, Wang Hongwen, Yao Wenyuan and Jiang Qing – who seized power in China on the death of Mao Tse-tung in 1976. Their few months in control were marked with the dogmatic insistence that their interpretation of Marxism was the one and only way forward. They backed up their beliefs with a brutal force that saw countless thousands of innocent Chinese imprisoned for daring to challenge them.

Less violent was the British 'Gang of Four' – Shirley Williams, Roy Jenkins, David Owen and William Rodgers – four MPs who broke away from the Labour Party in the late 1970s to form the Social Democratic Party. The party they founded was short-lived and eventually amalgamated with the Liberal Party, but its impact was enormous, forcing the Labour Party to reassess what it stood for and sowing the seeds that enabled Tony Blair to seize control of the party and to launch 'New Labour' in 1994.

Interesting perhaps, but these are not the gangs with which this book is concerned. The meaning of the word 'gang' in which we are interested is its principal one in the dictionary – 'a group of people who are associated together to act as an organized body...especially for criminal or illegal purposes'. This means, for example, the Mafia, the Triads and the other criminal groups who between them are responsible for most of the organized crime perpetrated in the world, and who control as much money as, if not more than, some of the world's largest economies.

These are the gangs that feature in the pages of this book: the gangs themselves, some of their most notorious members and the criminal underworld they dominate.

Gangs have been with us for centuries and history has given many of them a romantic hue. Robin Hood and his 'Merry Men' have come to be seen as a group of accidental outlaws dedicated to redistributing wealth from the rich supporters of the would-be usurper Prince John to the poor but loyal supporters of the true king, Richard I (who as it happened spent but a few months of his reign in England and spoke little or no English). The reality is rather different: any 'gang' to be found in Sherwood Forest would more than likely have been little more than footpads, probably quite happy to rob travellers for their own benefit, rather than that of the poor.

Ned Kelly and his gang have been promoted to the ranks of folk heroes in Australia. In reality, they were a gang of plundering thugs and murderers.

The James Boys, the Clantons and the other gangs that rode through the Wild West, their guns blazing, have attained legendary status thanks to countless Hollywood westerns. And similarly, the bootleggers who shot it out on the streets of Chicago and New York during the 'Roaring Twenties', and who have been glamourized in many movies, were among the most ruthless criminals who ever took aim and fired.

Welcome to Gangland.

Gangland crime is universal. There can be few, if any, countries in the world that are not affected by it in some way or other. Take Britain, for example. There, gangland crime is so rife that in July 2003, when addressing a criminal justice conference in London, the Prime Minister, Tony Blair, turned his attention to organized crime. 'Some have argued that the time has come to bring together some or all of the national law enforcement agencies which currently investigate serious organized crime...' he said, and went on '...and create a new dedicated national agency which could share intelligence, expertise and investigative talents'.

The review he proposed setting up involved looking at the roles of the National Crime Squad, the National Crime Intelligence Service and part of Customs and Excise. Officials were to be ordered to review current systems amid concerns in Whitehall that the various agencies' ability to tackle organized crime was damaged by rivalry, inefficiency and an overlap of activities. What was being proposed, in effect, was a British FBI, taking as its template the US bureau that has been at the forefront of the war against organized crime, not just in North America, but beyond its shores as well.

There was also, Blair announced, to be a review of the policing of points of entry into the United Kingdom, something that could result in a dedicated police force to deal with illegal immigration and smuggling. Both of these operations are widely organized by gangs. This applies especially to illegal immigration, whereby young men and women pay not just their life savings but also part of their future earnings to gangs who transport them from their homelands to the ports of Northern Europe and from there across the Channel or the North Sea into England. Many of these men and women apply for political asylum; others simply evaporate into their respective communities. They live not just in fear of being exposed and sent home, but in terror of falling foul of the gangs who brought them to Britain. Some even die in the effort; this fate befell a group of young Chinese crammed into an airtight container and driven onto a cross-Channel ferry. All but one of them suffocated to death in the process. Not that the gang that masterminded the operation cared: it had been paid.

After Blair delivered his speech, many people living in the peaceful, leafy suburbs of Britain asked why the United Kingdom needs a body such as the one the Prime Minister proposed to fight gang crime.

To answer that question…

There are reckoned to be 900 organized criminal gangs operating in the UK. Many of them are involved in drug trafficking, something that generates an estimated £8.5 billion a year. British gangs are involved in narcotics (as well as money laundering, fraud and revenue evasion) along with Colombian gangs who are mainly to be found in trafficking cocaine. Turkish-Kurdish gangs control the bulk of the trade in heroin, which comes from the Golden Triangle and Golden Crescent areas of Asia. West Indian Yardie gangs are heavily into drug trafficking, both smuggling illegal drugs into the country and selling them at street level. Albanian gangs control much of the vice in London and have more than a finger in illegal immigration. Chinese gangs are also heavily involved in this comparatively new crime of 'people smuggling' and in the age-old one of kidnapping. And West African gangs, especially those run by Nigerians, are heavily involved in fraud, particularly identity theft, one of the fastest-growing criminal activities in the early years of the third millennium.

Gangland UK has come a long way since the days when the East End was ruled by the Kray Brothers. Evil as they were, their escapades seem almost innocent by today's standards – although 'innocent' is not a word that anyone who found themselves on the wrong side of them would associate with Charlie Kray and the twins, Ronnie and Reggie.

At the top of the ladder are men who run their gangs with the same ruthless efficiency as successful industrial tycoons control their businesses, and indeed could easily be mistaken for them. On the lower rungs are small local gangs, involved in petty crimes, whose intense rivalry sometimes spills over into street violence, often with tragic results. At a New Year's Eve party in Birmingham in 2003, for example, two young women died and a third was gravely injured when they were caught in the crossfire between two rival gangs. Sadly, this was far from a one-off incident. Violent deaths of this sort are increasingly common on the streets of Britain.

There are, of course, gangs that are not involved in crime – or if they are, only at a very petty level. These street and school gangs strut the pavements and playgrounds they imagine that they control and can make life extremely unpleasant, indeed unbearable, for those they pick on, bullying and extorting small sums of cash from the seemingly weak and easily cowed. This can have tragic

Members of the California branch of the Hells Angels, Alameda, California.

consequences, evidenced by suicides of youngsters whose lives are made intolerable by those who pick on them. Often, members of these gangs graduate to full-time criminal activity, either on their own or as a member of a gang. This is especially true in the faceless public housing estates where such dissatisfied and often ill-educated youngsters are easy prey for the unscrupulous criminals who promise them a way out of their grim existence.

It's the same story in every country in the world. Wherever there's poverty there's crime, and wherever there's crime, there are men (and women) who organize it.

In Russia, Mafya gangs run the crime scene. There's an estimated three million hoodlums in five thousand gangs there. They make their presence felt in every Russian city, running prostitutes, the arms trade, drugs trafficking and white collar crime. They now operate in Israel, Hungary, the Czech Republic, and have muscled in on the US crime scene to the extent that Brooklyn's Brighton Beach is, in the words of one US lawman, 'the most notorious Russian satellite since Sputnik 1'.

In the United States, the Cosa Nostra still controls organized crime, despite a concerted effort by the FBI to bring the various 'families' to heel. They don't have the crime scene to themselves, though. Hell's Angels, based in California but with tentacles that reach into every state in the Union, deal in drugs, auto theft and prostitution, while Colombian and Mexican cartels vie with each other for control of the cocaine trade.

Japan's Yakuza gangs not only run pornography, money laundering, extortion and the usual gang rackets, but have infiltrated the highest strata of political life to the extent that it's difficult to tell who is in the Yakuza's pocket and who is on the level.

In Sicily, the Mafia is still *the* force to be reckoned with, its members running the island as if it was their own personal fiefdom – which it is. Across the Straits of Messina, in mainland Italy, it competes with Camorra gangs for primacy of the crime scene.

In Asia, the Triads and other gangs run the usual rackets, including the old-established trade in drugs smuggling. They have now added the newer one of human trafficking, taking hundreds of millions of dollars out of the heartless trade of smuggling people across international borders, and making it impossible for them ever to pay off the debt they owe.

Even in New Zealand, one of the most peaceful countries in the world, gang culture has hit the streets of Auckland and other major cities.

In South America, the Colombian drug cartels run a criminal empire that every year nets more than the combined yearly revenues of McDonald's, Kellogg's and Microsoft. The drug barons there are among the most arrogant criminals in the world. In its determination to kill two informants, one cartel is believed to have brought down Avianca Flight 203. The two informants died in the crash – along with the 105 innocent passengers and crew who were aboard.

*Busted in the jungle: Colombian national police destroy a cocaine laboratory
deep in the heart of the Colombian rainforest.*

Many of the gangs that we shall be looking at in the following pages are long-established and well-known criminal gangs such as Sicily's Mafia, the USA's Cosa Nostra, Japan's Yakuza and the like. Others, mainly Russia's Mafya, Jamaica's Yardies and South American drugs cartels are

'new kids on the block' but just as ruthless and well-organized as their older counterparts.

Street Gangs

We shall also be looking at a comparatively new phenomenon, street gangs. We say 'comparatively', although they have been around for more than a century. Many of them, such as New York's James Street Gang and similar ones in Chicago and other American cities, were the breeding ground for some of the most notorious criminals the world has ever seen. These include Al Capone and Johnny Torrio, both of whom made fortunes during the razzle-dazzle days of Prohibition in the United States.

As the 1900s unfolded there were very few cities that were not host to one street gang or another. Mostly they drew their members from the disaffected underclasses, who were housed in faceless, ill-designed housing estates, often situated some distance from the affluent suburbs but close enough to them for their prosperity to be seen and envied. As one section of society became more and more wealthy, another faced a life of low expectation and dependence on state benefits. It was from the youth of this section of society that street gangs mainly drew their members.

In the 1980s, youths from middle-class communities began forming their own gangs for the first time in US and European history. Even such traditionally staid countries as Switzerland started to experience the unprecedented appearance of these gangs. Their spread has witnessed an alarming rise in antisocial activities in many neighbourhoods, school playgrounds and college campuses in middle-class communities.

In the 1950s and '60s, street gangs could have been defined as loosely organized groups of individuals who collaborate for social purposes. Since the 1980s a more apt definition would be 'an organized group of individuals who come together for antisocial reasons'.

Such gangs usually have a leader or a cabal of leaders who issue orders and reap the benefit of the gang's illegal doings – muggings, shop-lifting, mobile phone theft and similar crimes – which not only fund the gangs' activities but increase their reputation on the streets. These crimes are often considered 'petty' by society, but not by those against whom they are perpetrated.

A gang may wear its 'colours', sport certain types of clothing, tattoos and brands, or imprint their gang's name or logo or other identifying marks on their bodies. Many gangs adopt certain hairstyles and communicate through the use of hand signals and graffiti on walls, streets, railway bridges, pavements, schools, and even on school assignments!

In large cities, small suburban gangs may identify with larger ones, or they restrict themselves to their own area or 'turf'. When splits occur or a new gang appears on the street, 'turf wars' can break out as the established gang fights off the threat to its superiority on the streets. The escalating use of violence in these wars is one of the most frightening aspects of 21st-century urban life. Guns are regularly used, not only by hardened gang members but also by

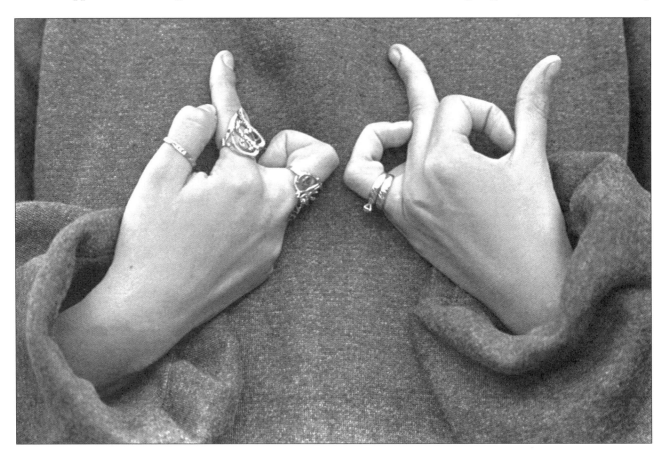

Female member of the Los Angeles street gang the Bloods shows off the hand signal that identifies her gang. The fingers spell out the word 'blood' from right to left.

youngsters scarcely into their teens and anxious to make a name for themselves on the streets.

A group of sociologists who have studied gang culture suggest that the following 'Three Rs' may help the layperson understand it better.

Reputation ('Rep') is of critical importance to members, who often refer to themselves as 'gangbangers'. Reputation extends to individual members and to the gang as a whole. Rep gives a gangbanger 'juice', and status within a gang is obtained by having it. The manner in which a gang member obtains his (or her) juice is as important as the juice itself. When a prospective banger is being 'interviewed' for gang membership, it is usual for them to embellish their pasts to impress whomever they are talking to. They will confess to crimes they haven't committed or blow up a minor role in some form of criminal activity into a more important one.

If a would-be member is considered to have enough rep to be admitted, he is often 'jumped in' – an initiation ceremony that involves him being 'beaten down' until the leader calls for it to end. If it's the young gangbanger who pleads for the blows and kicks to stop, then he obviously has neither the rep nor the juice to be a member. Those who do survive often join in a communal hug with existing members – an act of welcoming and of bonding.

From then on, the gang becomes the family, and with many youngsters who live in socially deprived areas that's the attraction of gang membership. It is a sad fact of modern life than many youngsters are raised in single-family homes where there is little or none of the family fellowship that most of us take for granted while growing up. And so, rejected or ignored by their parent(s) and often by their siblings who have problems of their own to cope with, youngsters are attracted by the camaraderie that the gangs offer and strive to gain the rep and juice to be accepted into the gangs' welcome embrace!

Respect is something everyone wants, but many gang members carry their desire for it to the extreme, not just for themselves but for the gang and its turf. Many gangs have a rule, written or unwritten, that rival gangs must always be treated with disrespect, or 'dissed'. If a gangbanger is seen by someone in his gang as failing to dis a rival gang, either verbally, in graffiti when the opportunity presents itself, or by staring down ('mad-dogging') a member of a rival gang when their paths cross, a 'violation' to other gang members might be issued. The guilty party can then find himself beaten down as punishment; should he offend again he will almost certainly be expelled from the gang. And as word on the streets spreads, his gang days are almost certainly over as his rep is in tatters and it is probable that he will never be accepted into a rival gang.

Retaliation demands that no challenge goes unanswered. Even something as trivial (to non-gangbangers) as being mad-dogged can result in whoever did the staring down finding himself the victim of a drive-by shooting or some other act of violent revenge. If a single member of a gang finds himself outnumbered by members of a rival gang, he loses no rep by running off, to return later with his 'homeboys' – members of his own gang who will help him bring the confrontation to some sort of conclusion.

(*Caveat*: gang vernacular can change with astonishing rapidity. A word or phrase that is in wide circulation one day might, the next day, be the language of the Moon as far as gang members are concerned. Some of the words used above are current at the time of writing: they may soon fall (or by the time of publication have fallen) into disuse and anyone using them would lose any trace of 'rep' they think they may have!)

When American composer Leonard Bernstein, at the behest of Jerome Robbins, was looking for a way of updating *Romeo and Juliet* and giving it musical form, he found his inspiration in the street gangs of New York. Juliet, the tragic young Capulet, became Maria, sister of the leader of the Puerto Rican Sharks, while the lovelorn Romeo was turned into Tony, the trying-to-go-straight former member of the native Jets. But the doomed lovers found there was no such thing as a former member of a gang. In one of the lyrics penned by Stephen Sondheim for the show, Riff, the leader of the gang, sings, 'When you're a Jet, you're a Jet all the way, from your first cigarette to your last dying breath.'

The words may be little more than the lyrics of a song written penned for a musical. But the message is very relevant to most gangs: once you're in, there's no way out!

Tony of the Jets (played by George Chakiris) holds a switchblade open, ready to fight a member of the rival Sharks gang in a still from the musical film, 'West Side Story,' directed by Jerome Robbins and Robert Wise, 1961.

THE SICILIAN MAFIA

A street in the Sicilian capital of Palermo, circa 1910.

THINK of organized crime. Think of gangs, gangsters and gangland, and the chances are that what come first to mind is the Sicilian Mafia. It is often called the Cosa Nostra ('Our Thing'), which is technically incorrect: the term was probably first used in the United States, coined by the FBI to distinguish the criminal activities of Italian-American gangs there from their Italian cousins. Founded in that mountainous, rugged island, probably in the late eighteenth or early nineteenth century, the Mafia now operates far beyond those shores. In Italy, in the United States, and in many other countries of the world, there are hardly any crimes in which the Mafia is not involved. Murder, prostitution, extortion, drug trafficking, smuggling, bootlegging: if there's money to be made from crime, the Mafia will be taking a cut of it.

Like so much of the organization, the origins of the name are shrouded in mystery. Some people believe it derives from the Arabic *mafia*, which means 'place of refuge', the island having been ruled by Arabs for the last two hundred years of the first millennium. Others believe it to be an acronym for one of two Italian phrases. The first is 'Morte Ai Francesi, Italia Anela' ('Italy wishes death to the French'). If true, this dates from the French invasion of the island in 1282. The alternative is 'Mazzini Autorizza Furto, Incendi, Annelenamenti' ('Mazzini authorizes thefts, arsons and poisonings'). Mazzini was one of the heroes of the unification of Italy, the nineteenth-century struggle to free the country from French and other countries' domination and to create one, unified state.

Banditry and murder were part and parcel of Sicilian life long before Mazzini and others began the struggle to create one Italian state with its capital in Rome. The Mafia developed largely as a result of social conditions of the island, which for the four hundred years before 1860 had been ruled successively by Spain, the Italian royal house of Savoy, the Austrian Hapsburgs and Spanish Bourbons.

It is thought that for several centuries the Mafia was a clandestine, patriotic resistance movement, carrying out guerrilla raids on occupying invaders. Gradually, it took over the role of mediator in disputes between landowners and peasant farmers, although their idea of mediating was indicative of the organization it was to become. Any move on the part of the peasants to form any sort of union was instantly quashed: and if the landlords didn't abide by the Mafia's decisions, their property was torched.

With the ending of feudalism, in 1812, many absentee landlords entrusted the running of their estates to administrators or gabellotti. They rented out parcels of land to tenant farmers, who were forced to hand over a percentage of what they grew or reared to the gabellotti. When the inevitable disputes broke out, it was to the Mafia that the peasants looked to for help; hence the popular misconception of the Mafia as 'Robin Hoods' and men of honour.

Each town or province had its own family of Mafiosi which came to be known by different names in different parts of the island – Fratuzzi (Brotherhood), Cudi Chiatti (Flat Tails), Mano Fraterna (The Brotherly Hand), and the Birritti (The Caps). Although the names may have varied, the way things were run was much the same in all parts of the island. A local don commanded each local family, members of each one swearing allegiance to him, and he, in turn, swearing allegiance to an overall don who lived in Palermo, the island's capital.

Then, as now, the code that bound the Mafia was omerta ('manliness' or 'silence'). Every member took a vow never to reveal Mafia secrets under pain of death. Betrayal was considered a crime on a level with the act of Judas, and neither church nor state was considered superior or held in more respect than the Mafia.

Young men, often little more than boys, who were destined for Mafia membership, were taught how to murder victims by sword, knife and garrotte. They were shown how to use torture in order to extract information from victims, how to use fear as a weapon and were fostered with a hatred for all authority apart from the Mafia and the Roman Catholic church. Secrecy was the organization's hallmark, fear and violent death its most trusty weapons.

In May 1860, Guiseppe Garibaldi (who, along with Mazzini and Count Cavour, was one of the three fathers of Italian unification) landed on Sicily, at Marsala in the west of the island, at the head of a force of a thousand men, which defeated the Bourbon army. Six months later, having declared himself dictator on behalf of King Victor Emmanuel (who was to become the first king of unified Italy), he held a referendum in which Sicilians voted for unification with Italy. The vote was controlled by the Mafia.

As the years passed, Italy became a land economically divided in two. The north, realizing the benefits to be gained from industrialization, prospered. The south, still dependent on peasant agriculture, stagnated. It was a land where banditry, cattle rustling, sheep stealing and extortion flourished. The *gabellotti* enclosed common pasture land and developed a protection system, using the Mafia to collect the payments. Anyone who refused to pay saw their livestock taken from under their eyes and driven into Palermo where it was sold to pay the 'debt'.

It wasn't long before the leading Mafia men, the dons, started looking at ways to extend their 'businesses'. They took control of the water supplies in the fertile land around Palermo, and then turned their attention to the city itself. Soon, they

were effectively running the fruit and vegetable markets, then the abattoirs and then many of the shops and small businesses.

Within a few years, there was hardly a single aspect of the economic life of Sicily that was not controlled by the Mafia. Beggars were forced to hand over part of their meagre takings in exchange for a 'licence' that guaranteed their pitches. Couples who got engaged and who, as custom dictated, went to church to light a candle to mark their betrothal, found that the only candles to be had were those sold by the Mafia. Victims of thefts, especially of jewellery, usually found that they were approached by a Mafia member who offered to get the stolen goods back – at a price.

Even the Church was not immune from the Mafia. Like modern-day ticket agents, local Mafia families bought seats in their neighbourhood churches, then rented them to church-goers.

In the early 1870s, Mafia leaders realized that while their various nefarious economic activities were making them exceedingly good livings, there was even more to be had if they took over the actual government of the island. In 1876, Raffaele Palizzolo ran for mayor in Caccamo. He won by a huge margin, although most of the voters had little option as to where to put their marks – gun-carrying Mafia members saw to that!

Within ten years, Palizzolo wielded political power over all of western Sicily, one hand in the government of the island, the other directing Mafia operations throughout his territory.

Another Mafia don who saw the plums to be had from being in national government was Francesco Crispi. Backed by Palizzolo, he stood for election as prime minister of the island – and with Mafia backing was duly elected. Taxes paid by the businesses he encouraged in his official capacity were looted by him from the national treasury to build up Mafia operations throughout the island.

By the turn of the twentieth century, the Mafia ruled the island. It brooked no opposition. Anyone who opposed them, usually members of the landed gentry or old-fashioned conservatives, was either ruined financially or, as happened to the Marquis Emanuel Notarbartolo, one-time director of the Bank of Sicily, eliminated. After publicly vowing to rid the island of the Mafia, Notarbartolo backed his words with money, funding anti-Mafia candidates at local and national elections. This was too much for the dons. In February 1893, the marquis was dragged from his private railway carriage and stabbed to death. His body was then badly mutilated and left on the railway track.

The investigation that followed showed just how deeply the Mafia had infiltrated the island's establishment. The man who replaced Notarbartolo at the bank was none other than Raffaele Palizzolo, who by now represented Sicily at the Italian Parliament in Rome, and who had been decorated by King Umberto I for outstanding civic services.

When the murdered man's son, Leopoldo, a serving officer in the navy, began to investigate his father's death, he was unexpectedly posted to the China Sea. Eventually, Mafia killer Guiseppe Fontana was charged with leading the gang who had murdered Notarbartolo. Magistrate after magistrate was appointed to hear the case. One by one, they proved unco-operative to the Mafia and one by one they were replaced until a Mafia-friendly one threw out the charges against him.

By now, Leopoldo had resigned his commission to dedicate his life to bringing to justice the men who had killed his father. Eventually, in 1899, Fontana was put on trial again along with the man accused of master-minding the murder – Raffaele Palizzolo. For over four years, during which the two men were held in prison, the legal proceedings dragged on and on. Witnesses mysteriously found that they had lost their memories. Damning documents that were there one day had vanished when they were called for in court. Palermo police refused to make vital documents available to the court, claiming they were not relevant to the case.

In July, 1904, after almost five years of being in prison, Fontana and Palizzolo were released. The Mafia ruled the island. There was not a police station, a military unit of the Sicilian army or any government office that it had not infiltrated. Anyone who tried to stand up to it was wiped out, often in full daylight in front of his family – a warning to others who had similar ideas.

Mussolini and the Mafia

When Mussolini swept to power in Italy in 1922, he sent one of his top police officials, Cesare Mori, to Sicily, charged to wipe out the Mafia. He soon realized the impossibility of his task. He rounded up and arrested

Cesar Mori, the 'Iron Prefect' despatched to Sicily by Mussolini, with orders to keep the Mafia under control.

suspected Mafia leaders all over the island. But when it came to their triials, there were few witnesses brave enough to give testimony, knowing that if they did so they would be killed, despite Mori's offer of police protection to anyone who would take to the witness box.

Realizing this, Mori, 'the Iron Prefect', simply left the suspected Mafia members he had arrested to languish in their cells for as long as he could; several years in many cases. In truth, though, the relationship between Mussolini's Fascists and Sicily's Mafia was that of one gang of criminals pitted against one another or, as one writer colourfully expressed it, 'two wolves fighting over the same chicken coop'.

Sicilian Mafia chief Don Calogero Vizzini, appointed Mayor of Palermo by the Allies.

Beyond Sicily

Long before Mori arrived in Palermo, the Mafia, all-powerful in Sicily, cast its eye beyond the island's shores, but its efforts at expanding its sphere of operations met with little

Gang boss I

success, in Europe at least. The long-established Camorra gangs, based largely in Naples, controlled crime in mainland Italy and were not going to cut their island compatriots into their operations. In Spain, France and other Mediterranean countries, the Mafia was forced to work with the gangs who ran things there and who were mainly concerned with drug trafficking and prostitution.

The Mafia was forced to look beyond Europe. And with so many Italians, including Mafia assassins

), wearing sun glasses, talks with his lawyer during a Mafia trial, February 1969

and thieves, emigrating to the United States, where better to cast the organization's criminal net?

Events in the United States during the Second World War had a profound effect on the post-war history of the Mafia and enabled it to maintain, indeed strengthen, its grip on Sicily.

One of the many thousands of Sicilian Mafia members who emigrated to the United States was Salvatore (better known as 'Lucky') Luciano. One of the legends of the criminal underworld, his tentacles extended into the US Navy with whom he established a lucrative relationship which probably made the Allied invasion of Sicily easier than it might otherwise have been. The task was made simpler by the fact that Cesare Mori's attempted enforcement of Mussolini's vendetta against the Mafia had made most Sicilians hostile to the Fascist cause, if not actively sympathetic to the Mafiosa. Thousands of Italian soldiers stationed at Lampedusa surrendered even before the invasion began, unwilling to risk their lives for what they knew to be a lost cause.

The post-war Mafia

Perhaps it was Lucky Luciano's influence with the occupying US forces; or perhaps it was that having been locked up for years by the Iron Prefect, it was easy for Mafia thugs to pose as anti-Fascist. Whichever was the case, it was members of the Mafiosa that the Allies installed as provisional mayors in towns and villages all over the island. When it came to being elected to office when the war was over, there was little opposition, and once again, the Mafia was in control of the island. The supreme head, or *capi di tutti capi*, was Calogero Vizzini, known to be a Mafia murderer, who was installed by the Allies as mayor of Villalba.

Until his death in 1954, Vizzini's men set about re-organizing the Mafia's activities, while at the same time, groups of independent bandits roamed the countryside, feared and resented by Mafiosi and innocent islanders alike. Ten thousand Sicilians attended Vizzini's funeral. The town he had ruled for so many years more or less closed down for eight days as a mark of respect.

Vizzini and his contemporaries had maintained, in public at least, a veneer of respectability and civility that could have allowed them to be mistaken for country squires, had not everyone known they were murderous thugs. In their own eyes, at least, they were men of honour, with their own code. And they restricted their activities to Sicily. The men who took over when Vizzini died, men like Genco Russo, Michele Greco and Luciano Liggio, were far from honourable, even by Mafia standards. They were *cafoni*, uncouth peasants, who lived by the gun (or the knife or garrotte). They rejected their predecessors' 'codes', preferring instead to adopt what old-fashioned Mafiosa derided as 'gangsterism' – the pursuit of money regardless of method or consequence. If the code of honour ever existed in Sicily, it vanished in a flurry of murders from which women and even children were not spared.

In 1957, the Sicilian Mafia re-established ties with their cousins in North America, which had become tenuous over the years. A few years later, during the 1960s, the Sicilian and American families united in their attempts to dominate the narcotics trade. This was despite the Sicilians' disdain for drugs; they believed that heroine and cocaine were somewhat 'less respectable' than extortion and murder – the Sicilian Mafia's traditional activities.

Of the two factions, the Sicilians were the more ruthless, often resorting to murder, not just of their own, but of judges and public officials whose activities they considered 'inconvenient'. Palermo's Falcone-Bersollino Airport is named in honour of two such judges, and in the same city there is a monument in Piazza 13 Vittimi at the end of the Via Cavour, dedicated to the memory of people killed by the Mafia.

In the capital, and in every other large city on the island, the Mafia gradually infiltrated the building trade and bribed their way into most government-run agencies. And if anyone wants to see the Mafia's influence, not on the island's criminal life, but on the way it impinges on countless thousands of Sicilians, all they have to do is look at the capital's housing estates. People

'The Six Roses', Sicilian Mafia leaders under house arrest on the island of Linosa near Sicily, 1971.

live cheek by jowl in depressing apartment blocks, crammed tightly together with no, or hardly any, green spaces and a remarkable lack of parking places for a people who love their cars and scooters. Why? Because nearly half of Palermo's public housing of the post-war years was built, albeit indirectly, by the Mafia. Salvo Lima, Palermo's mayor for many years, and his successor, Vito Ciancimino, who between them redefined the word 'corruption', sold building permits to Mafia-run companies, and there is little money to be made from the provision of parks and free parking places. And it wasn't only housing that suffered from Mafia involvement: Mafiosa controlled the city's beef market, and built and operated (still operate) several of Sicily's largest hotels.

The Mafia and the Church

The Catholic Church in Sicily has always had an uneasy relationship with the Mafia. While officially abhorring its activity, there is no doubt that many local priests have condoned, if not actively been involved in, Mafia activities. And not just at local level. Despite the fact that several priests who had spoken out against the Mafia had been murdered, with all the hallmarks thereof, in the 1960s, the Cardinal Archbishop of Palermo issued a statement that the Mafia has never existed.

There are many who believe that the Mafia's tentacles reach right to the heart of the Catholic Church – into the Vatican itself, citing as evidence the case of Roberto Calvi.

Calvi was the head of the Banco Ambrosiano, in which the Vatican had a substantial stake. It was also a bank that the Mafia used to launder much of the money they made from their illegal activities. Faced with the bank's mounting losses ($2 billion in the early 1980s), it appears that Calvi started to embezzle money from his Mafia paymasters to keep the bank afloat.

In June 1982, Calvi was found hanging under London's Blackfriars Bridge, with bricks and stones stuffed down his trousers and in his pockets.

'God's banker' Roberto Calvi, whose body was found hanging under London's Blackfriars Bridge, June 1982. Although a verdict of suicide was recorded at the time, many questions regarding Calvi's death remain unanswered.

A London coroner found initially that, faced with the collapse of his bank and with mounting debts, he had fled to London to avoid being sent to prison for fraud. A later inquest reached an open verdict.

Several *peniti* (informers) told the authorities in Rome that Calvi's death was no suicide. Mafia bosses, furious at the way that Calvi had mishandled the laundering of their money, had arranged for him to be killed. Calvi, sometimes known as 'God's banker' because of his Vatican connections, was lured to London, murdered and then hanged to make it appear that he had killed himself. The murder, several *peniti* claimed, was carried out by Francesco Di Carlo (Frankie the Strangler as he is known to his fellow mobsters), who was in London at the time.

In 2003, new forensic evidence, which had been garnered after Calvi's body had been exhumed a few years earlier, showed that the banker had not had any physical contact with the bricks and stones found on his body. New tests also showed that the marks on his neck were consistent with strangulation rather than hanging. In July that year, a panel of four Italian judges appointed to re-examine the case said they had no doubt that Calvi's death had been premeditated murder. They notified four men with supposed Mafia links, who were already under investigation for the murder, that they would be formally charged with the crime. One of the four was already in jail for Mafia-related crimes. Frankie the Strangler was not among them. He had always denied being involved in any way in Calvi's death, although he was extradited from Britain to Italy in its connection. Shortly after he reached Italy, Signor Di Carlo turned *penito*!

In reporting the Roman judges' decision to give the four accused men's lawyers time to present reasons why their clients should not be charged (something required under Italian law), the London *Times* said, 'The Vatican Bank, the Institute for Religious Works, suffered losses in the [Calvi] scandal, but their extent has never been revealed.'

The Mafia Today

So how does a criminal organization like the Mafia survive today? Note what activities it is involved in: extortion, protection, kidnapping, murders (down from 200 a year in the 1980s to just ten or so in the first decade of the third millennium), and, among its newer activities, dog-fighting! This used to be contained to Sicily until the 1980s, when it started to spread and become increasingly popular – and profitable to the Mafia, who make millions out of the accompanying betting, which they control. It is estimated that in Italy it is now a half-a-billion-dollar-a-year industry, and much of that goes to the Mafia. Any of about 40 different breeds (pit-bulls and Rottweilers are the favourites) are bred and trained for the sport, often by women and children who do it not just for money but also for the prestige that comes with owning a winning dog.

Training involves the dogs being kept hungry and then forced to pull weighted sledges towards food and

The European Parliament, Brussels, Belgium.

water, which strengthens their neck muscles. On fight days, the dogs are tied in a sack and beaten savagely before the neck is open and they are given sight of a small dog or maybe a cat. Furious and with a taste for their quarry they are released to face another dog, either an older one with a good fight record, or a stolen family pet. The fights, which can last from a few minutes to as long as two hours, go on until one of them is either too exhausted or badly injured to carry on, or has been killed (at least five thousand dogs die each year in these fights) by the other. The Mafia make money out of this 'sport' not by breeding winning dogs, but by

enemies, preferring instead to build networks. It is still involved in protection, as any director filming on the island knows only too well. When Giuseppe Tornatore was shooting *Malena* in Sicily in the late 1990s, he scoffed when told that unless he paid up, things would go awry. It was only after scenery was damaged by fire, costumes deliberately soiled and vital computer disks stolen from the production company's office, that Tornatore realized that the Mafia was not to be toyed with. In another case, Mafia members infiltrated the set as extras; no sooner had the director shouted 'Shoot!' than scenery started to fall over, the extras got in the way of the action and the director was forced to cut.

They are also into scams, such as the one operated by the *Cosa Nuova* in Naples where over three years sixteen thousand tons of artificial butter were made and sold as the real thing to bakeries and ice-cream manufacturers in Belgium, France and at home, in Italy. The scam yielded £30 million, half of which came from European Union subsidies.

The Mafia persists in Sicily for several reasons. High unemployment, a lack of confidence in the ability of the authorities to enforce the law, a widespread distrust of the state and the general secretiveness of the people all combine to enable organized crime to flourish not just in Sicily, but throughout southern Italy where ordinary people are often deeply suspicious of ordinary social forces. In Sicily, centuries of Mafiosa activities – kidnappings, extortion,

organizing the accompanying betting.

But to return to the question: how does a criminal organization like the Mafia survive today? They have adapted. The old-style Mafia has, to use a phrase coined by gangland expert James Morton, has evolved into the *Cosa Nuova* ('New Thing'), which has turned its back on making revenge killings et al – have encouraged the belief that everybody is 'at it'. Sicilians believe that their elected leaders are motivated by greed. Businessmen presume that their employees and associates will steal from them at the first opportunity. Union leaders presume that employers will exploit their workers as far as possible in order to line their pockets.

Mafiosi control the island's hotels, its transport, its banks and its construction industry. In a land without a tangible industrial base, everything has a price. There are few who cannot be bought, from politicians to bank managers and the men who run public utilities. Many

Former Italian Prime Minister Giulio Andreotti: was he a member of the Mafia?

public service jobs are sold, if not for money then for sex; with thirty per cent unemployment, smart attractive youngsters looking for a job are easy prey for the men with jobs to offer. Public contracts are usually awarded to whoever offers the highest kickback.

Throughout the island the Mafia mentality has encouraged an ethos where everybody expects a kickback. Sicilians call this mentality 'Mafiosit'. It doesn't mean that everyone is a Mafia member, it's just that they behave as if they were. And where widespread corruption is an accepted way of life, organized crime flourishes. Mafiosi may no longer rustle cattle, but millions of euros that flow into Sicily from the EU and other institutions reach their pockets rather than fund the development projects for which the mandarins of Brussels earmarked the money.

But perhaps the real reason for the Mafia's survival into the twenty-first century is that its tentacles reach into the very highest levels of political life, not just in Sicily but in Rome. In 1995 Giulio Andreotti, a former prime minister, was arrested and charged with being a member of the Mafia. True or not, even the fact that such a charge could be laid shows just how influential the Mafia really is.

But despite the fact that many Mafia members have now turned informer and that the evidence they have given has seen well over two hundred leading Mafiosa figures imprisoned in the last five years, the Mafia is too deeply rooted in the Sicilian way of life ever to be eradicated.

2 THE US MAFIA

*Immigrants to the USA welcomed by the Statue of Liberty
as they catch their first glimpse of the New York skyline, .*

THE story of the Mafia in America is one of two parts. The first covers the years when it was run by immigrants from Italy. The second is when they were supplanted by native-born Americans, many of whom came from Italian families, but who owed allegiance to the United States, looking to it for their future, rather than harking back to the good old days in Sicily.

America had seen gangs before. Anyone who has seen Martin Scorsese's box office smash hit, *Gangs of New York*, knows that. There were the Whyos, whose members specialized in contract beatings and murder. A straightforward punching cost $2, a broken jaw or nose came in at $10, and a broken limb $19. (Why they didn't round up to $20 no one knows. Perhaps like the men and women who set the price of things in our supermarkets, they realized that giving change for a paper note was good for business.) It cost $35 to shoot or stab someone in the leg or arm. And to kill someone cost $100. (They weren't fussy whom they killed but if the victim was an Englishman, all the better. Indeed it was rumoured that some Whyos who retained their Irish roots offered a discount in such cases!)

Then there was the Five Hand Gang, which ran the area bounded by Broadway, Canal Street, the Bowery and Park Row. One of the gang's leaders was Paul Kelly, a retired prizefighter who cultivated connections with the corrupt politicians who ran New York. This paid off when he was caught during one of the rare occasions when he personally committed a crime, something he did occasionally to impress his men. He was caught red-handed by the police and charged with robbery, a crime that carried a sentence of between ten and twenty years. A little pressure from above had the charge reduced to one of simple assault, for which Kelly served nine months in prison.

On his release, he founded the Athletic Association, an organization that, officially, provided recreational activities for the deprived street kids of New York. In fact, it was little more that an assortment of youth gangs, which Kelly directed for his own profit. One of the youngsters who joined was Johnny Torrio who went on to become a gang boss in New York, a crime overlord in Chicago and the elder statesman of organized crime in the US. During a fifty-year career in crime, Torrio established billion-dollar rackets, and ordered the deaths of countless mobsters. When Kelly recruited him he was a runt of a kid, who only joined the James Street Gang to avoid being beaten up by its members. But he was shrewd enough always to commit his crimes on his own. That way, he reasoned, no one could grass on him! Torrio so impressed Kelly that the old boxer encouraged him to form a youth gang of his own. It went on to include in its members two remarkable boys – Al Capone and Lucky Luciano.

The main difference between the two was that Capone had been born in the United States and Luciano in Sicily, which brings us back to the Mafia…

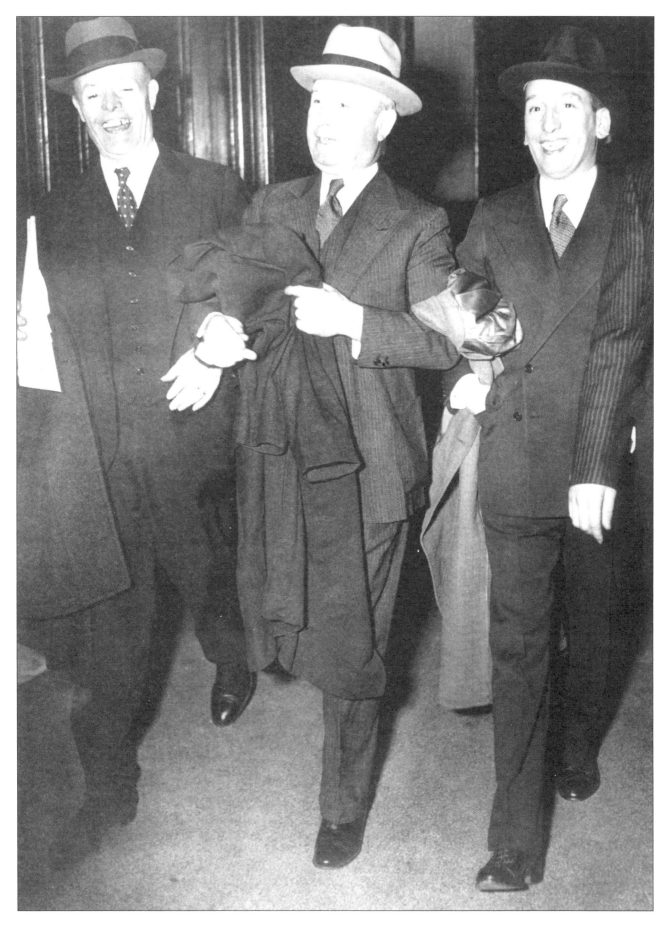

*Gang boss Johnny Torrio, arrested on charges of income tax evasion,
the same charges saw his gangster pupil Al Capone jailed for 11 years.*

Founded in Sicily, where it ruled the criminal roost for years, the Mafia's attempts to expand into other countries had met with little success. Mainland Italy had its own gang, the Camorra, which had held power probably for centuries. In France, Spain and other Mediterranean countries, the best the Mafia could hope for was to share the action with long-established local gangs. But the United States: here was the self-proclaimed land of opportunity, and when there were opportunities for profits to be made from crime, the Mafia were first in line.

In the 1880s, their stronghold was New Orleans. Historically French in outlook and with the sort of climate that reminded southern Mediterranean people of their homeland, the city had a well-established Italian-Sicilian population. It wasn't long after they started to put their roots down there that the Mafia had taken control of vegetable markets and dockside shipping, as they did back home in Sicily. And in the same way Mafia men were getting involved in local politics, to ensure their influence counted. They also brought with them their code regarding disloyalty. The first victim of an internecine Mafia murder in the US may well have been Vincenzo Ottumvo who complained that his share of the spoils was unfair and that if it didn't improve he would spill the beans. In the event it wasn't the beans that were spilled, but Vincenzo's blood: his throat was cut while he was playing cards.

French Quarter, New Orleans.

Within a few years, hundreds of thousands of Italian emigrants were leaving their homeland and crossing the Atlantic and settling in and around other major cities, especially New York and Chicago. Among them were countless Mafia members who brought with them the rackets that had yielded them so much back home – protection, extortion, prostitution, running the docks and markets, finding out which of the local police and politics had their price – and paying it.

Recruiting members was easy. Life was hard. The immigrants lived in terrible conditions in slum housing; their children roamed the streets lawlessly. There were schools, of course, but then what? A life of drudgery just like Mamma's and Papa's? Working round the clock for a pittance? The majority accepted their lot, worked hard: many of them prospered and within a generation or two had left the slums for other, more salubrious neighbourhoods. But others looked for the easy way out, and running with a gang – and in the Italian slums it was more or less certain it was a Mafia gang – provided quick bucks for little effort. Fine. And if being a gang member meant a life of crime and violence, theft and murder, that was fine, too. And if it meant that the main victims of these crimes were your fellow Italians, well, it's a dog eat dog world!

One of the scams the Mafia brought with them from 'the old country' was extortion, and the method they used was the Black Hand. It was practised in most US cities where there were 'Little Italies' – slum areas where

Italian immigrants lived. The method was simplicity itself. The target received a note demanding money on pain of physical violence or death. The letter was 'signed' with a crude black-ink palm print.

In his book *Gangland International* James Morton tells of the Black Hand letter that was received by a Brooklyn butcher in 1905. Written in a semi-literate hand it read, 'You have more money than we have. We know of your wealth and that you are not alone in the country. We want $1,000 which you are to put into a loaf of bread and hand to a man who comes in to buy meat and pulls out a red handkerchief.'

The man came into the shop, asked for meat, pulled out a red handkerchief and waited. Gaetamo Costa, the butcher, refused to pay. He was shot dead in his shop.

With such an example, it's not surprising that most people who received a Black Hand letter paid up. Although murders were rare, most of those who refused to pay were maimed. The dead can't pay, but the occasional killing served as an example. Shooting was the preferred method, but the garrotte, the knife, bombs and poison were also used.

One man who did pay was the Italian tenor Enrico Caruso, who parted with the $2,000 demanded if he wanted to avoid being poisoned. But when he was asked for $15,000 he went to the police who set up a trap and caught the extortionists. As it happened they were not Mafia members, just two petty criminals cashing in on the fear the Black Handers engendered among the

United States Federal agents throw 50-gallon drums of moonshine liquor
from the top windows of a house in Akron, Ohio, a large-scale illegal distillery.

Italian community. They were successfully prosecuted and from then on, Caruso was given police protection wherever he went; an internationally famous Italian was a natural target for a Mafia kidnapping.

It's said that by 1908 that for every Black Hand extortion that was reported, there were probably at least two hundred and fifty that went unreported. If this is correct then in that year alone there were over 100,000 Black Hand letters issued by Mafia and non-Mafia gangs. It was worst in Chicago where at least 80 Black Hand Gangs operated.

Within twelve years, the Mafia had more or less given up the Black Hand racket. In 1920, Prohibition was introduced. Alcohol was banned. And the Mafia saw the opportunities that bootlegging brought. As US writer Edward Dean Sullivan remarked, 'No work – slight risk – vast remuneration.'

When Prohibition began in 1920, existing liquor was locked away in bonded warehouses. Some of it found its way onto the flourishing black market through faulty paperwork: some was destroyed: some was given over to industrial use: and some was stolen by Mafia bootleggers. The trouble for them was that the bonded liquor wasn't going to last forever.

There were several solutions to the problem: bring it across the border from Canada or Mexico; ship it from Cuba and Europe; or make it. Home brewing and distilling was done in private houses and illegal dens all over the country, by people of every ethnic background, but in the Little Italies it was a Mafia operation.

In Chicago, for example, the *Unione Siciliane* via the Genna Brothers sold stills and ingredients to Italian residents and paid them for the hooch they produced. There was little choice in the matter. Any Italian who was known to be producing booze, even in small quantities for their own consumption, was called on by one or other of the six Sicilian immigrant brothers and their lieutenants.

The *Unione Siciliane* had been founded in the 1880s, ostensibly to provide insurance and to organize social gatherings for Sicilian immigrants in New York City. With its headquarters in Harlem, it soon became a political force, the Italian votes it controlled being able to swing elections in several city wards. Within a few years it had spread from New York into other major cities. With its Sicilian roots it was involved in the usual Mafia racketeering, prostitution, extortion, kidnapping and murder. Its members were a particularly unsavoury bunch even by Mafia standards: one of their early leaders is known to have burned alive in his basement six men who had got on his wrong side. He also had meat hooks installed in his office, from which he hung half-alive victims and made his gang watch their death throes as a warning of what lay in store for anyone who erred.

But back to Prohibition: in Cleveland, Italians were sold one-gallon stills and the ingredients by the Porello and Leonardos families. The finished product was bought by the same families and sold at the speakeasies they ran all over Ohio.

In Brooklyn, Frankie Yale, the

national president of the *Unione Siciliane*, controlled most of the homebrew business in his territory. Salvatore Maranzano was also a major player in New York's bootlegging business, not just in the city but all over the state, and into Pennsylvania.

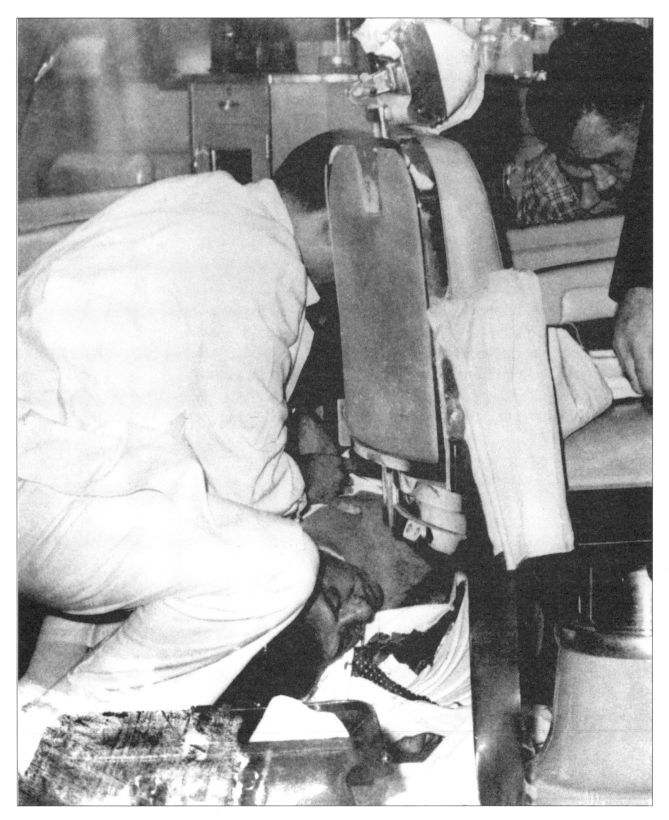

Albert Anastasia, reputed "Lord High Executioner" of the old Brooklyn Murder Inc ring, shot dead in a barber's chair in a New York hotel by unknown gunmen.

Across the country, in Denver's Little Italy, it was Jo Roma, boss of the city's family who ran the bootlegging business.

Prohibition saw a huge increase for foreign distillers. With coastguards and local police supplementing their salaries with bribes to turn a blind eye to booze coming in by sea or across the border with Canada and Mexico, Mafia families were able to bring in a huge amount of liquor. Officialdom lacked the manpower to do much about it, especially booze brought in from Canada, whose border with the United States runs for thousands of miles.

Liquor from Europe was often offloaded at Bermuda and St Pierre, a small island off the east coast of Canada, from where it was brought into the States by road from Canada, or by sea in the holds of small ships. More booze was unloaded at major ports where the Mafia not only had the right connections to make sure that the paperwork was in order, but where Italian stevedores unloaded the cargoes.

And with its insatiable eye for an extra profit, the Mafia was not happy with the huge profits that could be made selling the real thing. They diluted much of the liquor they brought in with water and simply rebottled it, or doctored it with industrial alcohol, rebottled it and relabelled the bottles. Scotch with names unheard of in Scotland, such as Prince Charlie's Sporran and other dreadful sobriquets, was swigged all over the States during the thirteen years that Prohibition was in operation.

Bootlegging was responsible for hundreds, probably thousands, of Mafia murders, as all over America gang fought gang for control of the lucrative trade. One of the first victims was Chicago's 'Big Jim' Colosimo who was gunned down in 1920 in his own restaurant by his own men who felt that he wasn't making the most of the opportunities Prohibition presented. In 1922, major-league bootlegger Dominic Scaroni was invited to dine at Niagara Falls by Canadian associates. It is said that he enjoyed the main course, but that he found the pudding hard to swallow as three bullets hit his head as he was eating it. One of the last victims of the Mafia's Prohibition days was Joe Roma who controlled Denver's homebrew industry. He was killed in an explosion by a rival gang.

The men who introduced Prohibition into the USA could have had no idea that one of the indirect consequences was that the various Mafia families, who until then had had little to do with each other, now bonded together in crime. If the Mafia in one city wanted to deal with bootleggers in another, it would be with the local Mafia family they would deal rather than one of the Jewish or other bootlegging gangs.

By 1931, relations with more than 20 Mafia families were formalized and in that year a group of the big time bosses got together and established a forum – the Commission – to arbitrate on inter-Mafia matters.

It was decided that the Commission should be composed of seven members – the bosses of the big gangs

– and that those families without seats on the Commission would be represented by a member who was. Membership of the Commission lasted for five years when the next 'Board Meeting' was held. Interim meetings were held to discuss any pressing matters. (At the 1956 meeting, it was decided to increase the number of members on the Commission to nine, starting in 1961.)

The Commission's word was backed up with an armed enforcement branch, which became known as Murder Inc. Under the rules, Murder Inc killed only for pressing 'business' reasons, and was never to be brought into action against outsiders, such as politicians, prosecutors or reporters. Killing such figures would interfere with the Cosa Nostra's ability to bribe important contacts.

No one knows how many murders the organization was responsible for until it started to unravel in 1940, when one of its members, Abe Reles, was arrested along with other lesser mob members. Reles decided to sing. As a result of the information Reles, 'The Canary of Murder Inc', gave to the police several men went to the electric chair. He died when he 'fell' from a window in the Coney Island hotel where he was being held under 'failsafe' police protection.

The Commission regulated (and still does in New York) much of US Gangland. A major league gangster who overthrew his boss could only hope to survive if it the Commission gave its blessing, as happened in 1951 when Albert Anastasia had his boss Vincent Mangano, a Commission member, shot. He was hauled before the Commission and pleaded that he had acted in self-defence. This claim was backed up by the boss of the Genovese Family. The Commission accepted this and Anastasia was appointed to his old boss's place on the Commission.

By imposing this sort of discipline on its members, the Commission hoped to avoid the feuds and internecine gun wars that had brought the Mafia such bad publicity during the years of Prohibition. Sadly, it didn't save Anastasia. Six years later, in October 1957, when he was having his hair cut, gunmen burst into the barber's shop and shot four times in a classic gangland slaying. No one was ever charged with the murder.

Many Americans assumed that the gangster era had come to an end when the Prohibition laws were repealed. They were in for a shock when a week or two after Albert Anastasia had been assassinated New York State police raided a house in upstate New York when they were tipped off that 58 underworld leaders were meeting at the mansion belonging to one of their number, Joe Barbara. It turned out that the gangsters didn't come only from New York: they hailed from Florida, Texas, California, Illinois and Ohio as well as New Jersey and Pennsylvania. As soon as the police appeared, many of the men escaped into the woods surrounding the house; others were detained.

What became known as the Apalachian Conference galvanized the FBI into starting to crack down on

Joseph Valachi, mafiosi turned informer, testifies before the Senate Rackets Committee in Washington, October 1963.

Mafia activities. For years, FBI boss J. Edgar Hoover had been denying that the Mafia was active in the US: indeed, he did not even accept that there was organized crime in the country at all.

When news of the Apalachian Conference got out, he could no longer make that claim. By that time, the Mafia was in control not just of much of the organized crime in the States; Mafia men were running American unions, they more or less owned Las Vegas, which had been built with Mafia money. They controlled gambling – on and off-track betting, the numbers racket and slot machines. They were big in drugs trafficking, although according to strict Mafia rules, narcotics is not something they should be involved in. Mafia men ran brothels all over the country and were quick to move into pornography. Later, when credit cards started to be widely used, they were quick to see the opportunities for fraud they represented. Several families made millions out of stock and bonds, buying at a low price and using high-pressure (often a euphemism for strong-arm) tactics to get others to buy the stocks they had invested in. The increased demand drives up the price, and when the Mafia men think they have driven the price as high as it will go, they are the first to sell. The vast amount of stocks they offload, having made a huge profit, sends the price plummeting, never to rise again, leaving the men who had been persuaded to invest to count their losses.

From 1957, the FBI began a massive intelligence-gathering operation focusing their efforts on the Cosa Nostra, and when Robert Kennedy became Attorney General in his brother's administration in 1961, he declared that the Cosa Nostra was a prime target for the resources of the US Justice Department. He scored a coup in 1963 when a low-ranking Mafia member Joe Valachi testified before a Senate committee investigating organized crime in the States, outlining the structure of the Mafia and naming names.

Between 1963 and 1970, the FBI leaked details to selected reporters about the men they knew were running some of the various Mafia families. The stories the journalists filed fuelled media and public interest in the Cosa Nostra and turned up the heat. But still the Mafia continued to operate. Between 1967 and 1970 Carlo Gambino of New York and Anthony Accardo of Chicago emerged as the two most powerful Mafia men in the United States. Also between these years the US Congress passed the Omnibus Crime Control Act (1968) and the Organized Crime Control Act (1970) which, along with the Racketeer Influenced and Corrupt Organization Act (RICO), were to prove instrumental in crippling the Mafia for much of the 1980s. A programme was also introduced to offer protection to witnesses.

There were a few teething troubles, but after FBI agent Joe Pistone infiltrated the Bonanno Family, one of the 'Big Five' that had carved up the crime scene in New York for decades, and showed how the RICO act could be used against entire families, the FBI spearheaded a massive assault on the Cosa Nostra, beginning with a huge intelligence-gathering operation was started, with local and state police coast to coast involved. The RICO Act began to be widely used and started to hurt Mafia families badly, and put many non-Mafia gangs out of business.

But the Mafia wasn't (and still isn't) finished. Cocking a snook at the FBI in 1985 when they were bringing major racketeering cases against New York's 'Big Five' (the Bonanno, Colombo, Gambino, Genovese and Luchese Families), John Gotti of the Gambinos eliminated rivals for the capo position in spectacular fashion. He ran the Family until he was eventually sent down for life in 1992. Such was his popularity that on the day he was sentenced, a thousand people crowded the sidewalk outside the courtroom, chanting, 'Free John Gotti' and 'Freedom for John'.

His son John took over, but he was arrested and pleaded guilty to charges of telecommunications and con-struction fraud, racketeering, loan-sharking and extorting money from a Manhattan nightclub. The betting was that the Number One position would pass to his brother, Peter. In the Family, family is everything.

The Gottis, father and son, joined and have been joined by a host of other Mafia leaders to be put away, many of them, like John Junior, pleading 'Guilty' in exchange for a reduced sentence. In the past twenty years of so, more than 25 Mafia bosses have heard the doors of their prison cells slam behind them and known that it would be a long time before they would be free.

Even so, the US Mafia is still *the* major force in US organized crime. Mafia families continue to operate the traditional Mafia rackets, but many of the mobsters have started to invest the proceeds of their crimes in legitimate business, something that makes tracking them down a problem for the FBI.

The fight against the Mafia in the US is an ongoing one. There will always be men on both sides of the law, and for every college graduate who applies to join the police or FBI, there will be at least one young hoodlum, probably with an Italian-sounding name, desperate to make the grade into his local Mafia family. To do so, he may have to prove himself willing to kill for the mob. He may have to swear an oath. He will have to swear to do whatever is asked of him. He must promise never to inform on a fellow member. He must always show the utmost respect to the wives and girlfriends of other Mafiosi. He will have to agree to ask permission before doing deals, or leave the area, even for a short time. He will be told not to get involved in disputes with other members of the Family. (Inevitably such disputes do break out, and when they do, both parties are summoned to a 'sitdown' where they are read the riot act and forced to shake hands.) He will be told not to get involved in drugs trafficking, although this is usually taken to mean he will not get caught being involved in drugs trafficking.

And he will be told what the penalty is for breaking the Mafia code. Death!

3 US MAFIA ROGUES' GALLERY

THERE were and are literally thousands of members of the US Mafia. Some are the big-time gangsters who were the role models for many Hollywood movies, starring amongst others George Raft, the archetypal Hollywood mobster and who was himself refused a work permit in Britain because of his Mafia connections. Others are the petty

New York's Brooklyn Bridge, connecting sleek downtown Manhattan with rough, tough Brooklyn.

gangsters at the bottom of the pile – the soldiers whose muscle, knives and guns are at the beck and call of the lieutenants to whom they owe absolute loyalty. It would take a book many times the size of this one to detail the lives of all the top men in American gangland. Carl Sifakis's *Mafia Encyclopedia* and Jay Robert Nash's *World Encyclopædia of Organized Crime*, two hefty tomes, both detail the lives, times and crimes of many of them. Jo Durden Smith's *Mafia* is a good introduction to the topic. Here, we restrict ourselves to three individual Mafia men, one Family and perhaps the most famous US gangster of all time who, despite popular opinion, was never a Mafia member – indeed he loathed the Cosa Nostra and every one of their number, although that didn't stop him doing business with them.

Al Capone

At the end of January, 1947 a small, family funeral was held at Chicago's Mount Olivet Cemetery. Just one burial among several held that day, and nothing unusual about it.

Nothing unusual, that is, apart from the fact that when the casket had arrived in Chicago from Florida where the deceased had spent his last years, it was met by armed guards. And nothing unusual apart from the fact that a few days after the ceremony, the coffin was dug up and reburied in a secret plot in Mount Carmel Cemetery, so afraid were the deceased's grieving family that grave robbers would abduct the corpse.

The name on the brass plaque screwed on the coffin was Alphonse Caponi. He was better known to the world as Al Capone, although few who had known him in his prime, would have recognized the shambling, rambling syphilitic wreck as the man who two decades before had ruled Chicago,

Al Capone was born in New York's Brooklyn in 1899. His parents, Teresa and Gabriele Capone, had come to America six years before from Naples. If anyone ever made the mistake of saying in his presence that Capone had been born in Italy, he would roar that he was not Italian, 'I was born in Brooklyn.'

He and his eight brothers and sisters were raised in a seedy four-room apartment, his parents (his father was a barber), like other Neapolitan immigrants exchanged the slums of Naples for the slums of New York. By the time Al was eleven, he was as streetwise as a many a petty criminal twice his age. He was quick to learn from older members of the gangs he ran with and by the time he was in his teens he was an adept knife-fighter and could handle a revolver with the best of them.

The first gang to which Capone swore allegiance was the Bim Booms one of whose members was Charles Luciania, later to gain notoriety in his own right as 'Lucky' Luciano, one of the most vicious gangsters the United States has ever seen. (He changed his surname to avoid embarrassing his family when his name started to appear in the newspapers in connection with the crimes he committed.) The two went to the same school in Brooklyn where Capone's attendance record and grades were better than ordinary until the call of the streets got to him and he began to truant.

Every day on his way to school, the young Al passed the headquarters of Five Points Gang, an outfit that was run by Italian gangster Johnny Torrio The Five Points was one of the most powerful gangs in New York with 1,500 thugs on call to rob, extort money by any means and murder whomever they were told to!

Capone's schooldays came to an end one day when he was given a dressing-down by one of his teachers: thoroughly humiliated by the experience he knocked the teacher to the floor. The headmaster burst into the classroom and thrashed Capone. He ran from the building and never went back.

He got a job in a bowling alley and a sweet shop, and took to hanging round pool halls and became a successful hustler. Within a few months he had graduated from the Bim Boomers to the Five Pointers in much the same way that a twelve-year-old goes from primary to secondary schools: having learned the basics, time to broaden the mind!

At first Capone was just another kid in the Five Pointers, but when he was fifteen he found out that the Mafia's Black Hand Gang had been extorting money from his father. Perhaps this was the genesis of his hatred for the Mob, perhaps he had

The most famous gangster of them all: Al Capone, seen here in the company of US Marshal Laubenheimer (l), circa 1930.

come to loathe them before that. Whatever, Capone was so angry that he hunted the two men who had threatened his father and shot them dead.

This impressed Torrio who gave Capone the job first of beating up loan-shark victims who got behind with their payments, then as a pimp, beating up girls who were suspected of holding back some of the money they made. When he wasn't working he was honing his skills with revolver and automatic pistol, shooting at empty beer bottles in the basement of the Adonis Social Club, which was run by Joe Adonis, who went on to become a big-league mobster in his own right.

After a year or two working as a Torrio enforcer, Capone was given a real job in the organization, as a bouncer in Harvard Inn, run by an associate of Torrio's, Frankie Yale. Torrio himself moved on to pastures new, forsaking New York and making his headquarters in Chicago.

In 1919, Torrio was busy establishing his bootlegging empire in the city. The Volstead Act that was to bring prohibition to the United States had started its journey on to the statue book, and Torrio had been

George 'Bugs' Moran, circa 1938.

quick to see the opportunities this would bring.

He was not alone

Torrio's gang, which controlled the south side of Chicago, was one of twelve in the city that supplied booze to the city's drinkers, who seemed to have had an insatiable thirst for the stuff. The inner West Side was supplied by the Druggan-Lake gang, a particularly nasty mob of Irish thugs. But they weren't the most vicious: that dubious honour went to the West Side's Gennas, six brothers from Sicily who killed both for gain, for self-protection – and for kicks.

The other big player in Chicago's gangland was the mob run by failed safecracker and successful florist Charlie Dion O'Bannion. A devout Catholic, O'Bannion kept a flower shop across the street from the Holy Name Cathedral. The shop served as both a legitimate business and the front for the gang he ran with fellow former altar boys, George 'Bugs' Moran and Hymie Weiss, a man so devout that he never went out without a rosary and a crucifix on his person, along with a gun. The O'Bannion gang was the biggest challenge to Torrio's dominance.

There was little trouble to begin

with – demand for illicit liquor was so high that there was plenty of business for everyone involved in supplying it. But within a few months things began to change: bootlegging operations were being run on a much slicker basis and inter-gang rivalry saw opposing mobs trying to muscle in on each other's territories and operations.

When trucks loaded with John Torrio's beer were hijacked and his speakeasies were attacked, his men retaliated by having the men suspected of being responsible eliminated.

'Divide and rule' is a motto that has served many men well. And seeing the opportunities that the Chicago underworld internecine struggles presented, Torrio decided that the time was right to fulfill his ambition and take overall control of the city. Extra muscle would be needed, and Torrio remembered the young thug who had impressed him so in New York.

By this time Al Capone was 25 and high up in the Five Points Gang hierarchy. He had a bright future on the New York crime scene, but the offer Torrio made him was almost unbelievable – a quarter of all existing turnover and half of all new business in exchange for Capone's services in Chicago.

It wasn't long after he arrived in the Windy City before he had claimed his first victim – a very small fish, called Joe Howard, in the big pond of Chicago gangland. The night after he had organized the hijacking of two of Torrio's trucks, both of which were loaded with hooch, someone pumped six bullets into him as he was enjoying an illegal drink. The 'someone' was Al Capone.

The Chicago Police Department was by now so used to internecine gangland crime that the men who went to investigate Howard's killing were hardly surprised to learn that even though the bar where the killing had happened had been busy, no one appeared to have seen anything. Even so, the police pulled Capone in for questioning, but with no evidence against him were forced to release him.

By a combination of bribery and intimidation, Capone set about making sure that there would be no police interference in his activities. From his headquarters in the Hawthorne Inn Cicero, one of the city's middle-class suburbs, he was soon running an empire of brothels, speakeasies and gambling dens. It was a 24-hour, seven-day-a-week operation. There were few challenges from officialdom. The men he hadn't bought were too scared to try to stop him. Within two years of leaving New York, Capone was making at least $100,000 a week.

Not content with the fortunes they were earning from the territory they controlled and operations they ran, Capone and John Torrio cast their eyes on other parts of the city. The younger man took a different view of things from his mentor on how to bring the entire city under into their fiefdom. Capone wanted to embark on a short winner-take-all war. Torrio preferred to play a waiting game, holding his fire until the time was right.

That time came at the end of

October 1924, when Dion O'Bannion's gang hijacked a shipment of Canadian whiskey destined for the Genna Brother's speakeasies. When one of O'Bannion's men, Hymie Weiss, advised O'Bannion to make show some contrition, Dion said, 'Oh, to hell with them Sicilians.'

His words were a declaration of war!

A few days later, on November 4, Dion O'Bannion was gunned down in his flower shop. The three gunmen responsible had to push their way across the busy sidewalk to get to their waiting car, but no one in the crowd was able to give the police anything more than the sketchiest of descriptions, indeed most in the crowd claimed to have seen nothing.

The police rounded up Al Capone, Johnny Torrio and the six Genna brothers but had to release them when their alibis checked out.

Among the hundreds of lavish floral tributes that accompanied O'Bannion's casket as it was driven from the chapel of rest to the cemetery was a basket of beautiful red roses from Al Capone. He attended the funeral along with Johnny Torrio and the rest of Chicago gangland and 100 of the city's police, there to keep the peace.

When a reporter asked Hymie Weiss if he thought Capone was responsible for O'Bannion's murder, Weiss, who had shed real tears all the way through the service, threw back his hands in horror and said, 'Blame Capone? Why Al's a real pal. He was Dion's best friend, too.'

No one was fooled. In the coming months Weiss sent his gunmen to get

Capone and Torrio. Capone escaped unscathed. The first attempt on Torrio's life saw his chauffeur and dogs die in a hail of bullets, and left Torrio with two bullet holes in his Fedora.

The second attempt on Torrio would have succeeded had the two gunmen not been scared off by an

approaching laundry van as they were about to shoot him in the head at point-blank range after he had been felled by a sawn-off shotgun. He recovered, but no sooner was he out of hospital than he was arrested for running an illegal brewery and was sent down for nine months. When he came out, he announced he was leaving Chicago. 'It's too violent,' he said, as he prepared to pack his bags for a long vacation in the Mediterranean.

Capone escorted Torrio and his wife to the station and installed bodyguards in the compartments on either side of their lavish, art deco stateroom on the *Twentieth Century*,

With prohibition in full swing, Federal officials destroy barrels of whiskey, under the gaze of a distinctly non-committal public.

one of the most famous trains of the day. When the guard ordered those who were not travelling to leave the train, Capone turned to Torrio, embraced him and said, 'So long, Johnny Papa. You come back when you feel better.'

'It's all yours, Al,' Torrio said.

At the age of 26, Al Capone, the son of impoverished Italian immigrants, found himself running an empire of thousands of speakeaseies, brothels, breweries, rackets of all sorts, all of which brought in around $50 million a year.

Not long afterwards three of the Genna brothers were gunned down over a period of six weeks. The other three sailed for the safety of Sicily. Capone always protested innocence of the killings of Angelo, Mike and Antonio Genna: they were his allies. The man most people suspected of getting rid of the Sicilian brothers was Hymie Weiss. There was also the little matter of revenge for the slaughter of Dion O'Bannion.

In August 1926, Weiss and his men trailed Capone from his home in Prairie Drive to one of his gambling clubs, the Four Deuces. As Capone got out of the car, Weiss's men opened fire, killing the driver, Tony Ross, but missing Capone, who somehow managed to get behind the wheel and drive the car straight through the club's front door.

A few weeks later, customers in the coffee shop of Capone's Hawthorne Inn were terrified when someone fired a sub-machine gun through the window. Capone went to investigate, but was hauled to the ground by one of his bodyguards, Frank Rio.

'It's a trick, boss,' Rio said.

He was right. Moments later a fleet of gangster-filled cars screeched to a halt outside Capone's headquarters in Cicero. By the time they roared off a few minutes later, the fifty gunmen had raked the building with more than 5,000 bullets from guns, hand-guns and machine-guns. The coffee shop was a wreck.

Incredibly none of the people having lunch in the coffee shop were injured. The sound of the first gunshots had seen them flying to the ground – and staying there for the duration. One family, on holiday from Louisiana were not so lucky. They had just parked their car when the shorts started to fly. One bullet went through the driver's hat. Another grazed his son's knee and a third hit his wife in the arm. Worse, bullets slammed into the windscreen shattering, sending lethally sharp shards flying in all direction, one of which hit the petrified Louisiana woman in the eye, coming close to blinding her.

Capone paid for all the damage to the cars that had been parked outside, and settled the $10,000 hospital bill to save the Louisiana woman's sight.

For one of the rare occasions in his life, Capone was frightened. His life had been threatened in his own stronghold, the one place where he felt absolutely secure.

Hymie Weiss had to go.

Three weeks later Weiss was gunned down as he was leaving the Holy Name Cathedral, heading for his headquarters above the O'Bannion flower shop.

Hymie's widow was understandably devastated. Not just at her devoted husband's death, it was rumoured, but at the fact that her husband rated only eighteen cart-loads of flowers at his funeral, far less than O'Bannion and many of the other gangsters who had been gunned down in the gang wars blazing all over Chicago!

A few days after Hymie Weiss had been slain, Capone called a meeting at the Hotel Sherman attended by the remaining Chicago gang bosses, including Bugs Moran, the only man big enough to challenge him for the Number One position in the Chicago Underworld. Capone proposed that the city be divided among them. There was plenty to go around. Capone is believed to have controlled ten thousand speakeasies, the proceeds of which along with money from the brothels he owned and gambling rackets he ran, were earning him around $300 million a year. He had his expenses though. The thousands of dollars he spent on hand-sewn silk shirts, hand-lasted shoes, bespoke pin-stripe suits and diamond tie pins paled in comparison to the £30 million he spent buying policemen, judges and politicians.

Everyone in Chicago knew he was a gangster, but few cared. He made millions out of bootlegging, but to most people the Prohibition laws under which they flourished were nonsense. And if there were gun battles on the streets of Chicago, it was gangster v gangster: very few 'civilians' were injured. And Capone made sure that his donations to charities and other good causes were

far from anonymous.

For a while the truce that Capone proposed in the aftermath of Hymie Weiss's death held. Even so, Capone decided that Chicago was no place to bring up the family to which he was devoted and in 1928 he bought a large mansion in Miami.

With Capone in Florida, Bugs Moran decided to take advantage of his absence. First of all his North Siders started to hijack trucks carrying Capone liquor: then they started to muscle in on the dry-cleaning and other above-board businesses Capone operated.

Two or three weeks into 1929, from his Florida mansion, Capone telephoned his number-one in Chicago, Jake Guzik, and told him that Moran had to be removed from the scene. February 14 – St Valentine's Day – was the date chosen, more then enough time for Capone to fix an appointment with a well-respected Miami city official for that day. Capone wanted a watertight alibi from an unimpeachable source.

Capone's men set up Moran's mob, by having a Detroit gangster who was on Capone's payroll, offer Moran a consignment of liquor he claimed he had hijacked from Capone. Moran jumped at the bait and arranged to take delivery of the booze at 10.30 am on St Valentine's day at a garage at 2122 North Clarke Street.

At the appointed time, when Capone was safely at his Miami meeting, several of his gangsters dressed as policemen rushed into the garage. Inside, six of Moran's most trusted men were waiting, waiting to take delivery of the liquor. Moran

The hit: bodies of members of Bugs Moran's gang lie dead in the bloody aftermath of the St Valentine's Day Massacre.

would have been there, had he not overslept. He was just about to arrive at the scene, with two of his lieutenants, when he saw what he took for policemen going inside the garage. Assuming it was just another police raid, the three of them slipped into a coffee shop to wait until it was over. When they heard gunshots echoing from the garage, they hotfooted it to safety (Moran would eventually die of cancer in prison in 28 years later, serving a ten-year sentence for bank robbery).

A few moments later a witness who lived across the street saw two men coming out, hands in the air, with two policemen behind them. The quartet, who were in fact Capone's men, got into a Cadillac and drive off. Curious, the woman ran over to the garage and saw the carnage – seven blood-smeared men sprawled on the floor among the oil patches and other garage detritus.

Six of the men were pronounced dead on arrival at hospital. One of them, Frank Gusenburg, was still conscious, but he died three hours later, true to the curious honour that existed among Chicago gangsters, refusing to say a word.

Moran was not so reticent. When he was hauled in for questioning he said, 'Only Capone kills like that.' The remark was widely reported, but Al Capone had a watertight alibi.

People not just in Chicago, but all over the United States were horrified at what came to be known as 'The St Valentine's Day Massacre.' It marked a turning point in public opinion. The swashbuckling prohibition-bustin' bootleggers were now widely regarded as the cold-blooded killers they were.

Despite the about-turn in public opinion it was cocky Al Capone who returned to Chicago, confident that he had crushed any challenge to his authority to his mastery of the city's crime scene. But not long after he got there he learned that two of his must trusted men, John Scalise and Albert Anselmi, were in league with another Chicago gangster, Joseph 'Hot Toe' Guinta, and were planning to eliminate him. At first he refused to believe it, but when a trap was laid for Scalise and Anselmi and the accusation was proved to be true Capone decided to act.

He invited the two turncoats along with Guinta to be guests of honour at a banquet at the Hawthorne Inn. According to gangland legend, Capone made was halfway through a speech about the importance of loyalty when he casually wandering around the room until he had positioned himself behind the three plotters. At this point he is said to have laughed, 'I understand you want my job. Well here it is.' As he spoke he was handed a sawn-off metal baseball bat, which he brought

Al Capone (centre) hides his face as he leaves the Federal Building in Chicago, surrounded by his friends and bodyguards, after being interviewed regarding his income tax situation.

down on their heads, smashing their skulls. As they slumped forwards, their faces coming to rest in the plates of still-warm pasta in front of them, Capone took a revolver from his pocket and delivered three coups de grace. As a lesson to others, he ordered every bone in their bodies broken. The bodies were found just across the state border with Indiana, two draped across the seats of a car, the third dumped in a ditch.

A month after the St Valentine's Day Massacre, Herbert Hoover was inaugurated as US president, largely on a law and order ticket, and bent on jailing Al Capone.

It wasn't just the authorities that were starting to give Capone a bad time. In May the same year he attended a meeting of the US's top criminals, chaired by his old mentor, Johnny Torrio. The meeting had been called to introduce them to Moses Annenberg, whose wire-service was to be used to control racing results throughout the country. But as well as welcoming Annenberg into their cartel of crime, the other gangsters there turned on Capone, claiming that the St Valentine's Day had been, to put it politely, ill-conceived. (In one memorable gangster B-movie, which featured the meeting, one of the men turns to the actor playing Capone and says, 'Bad for PR, Al. Bad for PR.')

Worse was to come. Later that month and still smarting from the criticism he received in Atlanta, he was tipped off that Bugs Moran had put a $50,000 price on his head. Capone decided to go to a place of greater safety and where safer than

prison. Using contacts in the Philadelphia police department he contrived for himself and Frank Rio, his most trusted lieutenant to be arrested leaving a cinema in the city and charged with carrying firearms.

He was sentenced to a year in prison, and in the event served ten months, getting two month's remission for good behaviour. Prison life wasn't too bad for Capone and Frank Rio. He managed to keep tabs and run his criminal empire from his cell: the other prisoners were in utter awe of him, so were the warders! And he was safe from the assassin's bullet.

When he was released he found things were changing. In politics when it is perceived that the all powerful could be loosing their grip even a little support starts to ebb: at first a trickle, then a stream and by towards the end a torrent, as when the seemingly invincible Margaret Thatcher started to look vulnerable, she lost her power base and the prime-ministry in a remarkably short time.

As in politics so in crime.

The St Valentine's Day Massacre had turned public opinion and against him and had cost him the support of his fellow crime barons. There was a president in office who wanted Capone dealt with. Now, out of jail, the supremo of Chicago gangland lost the support of the journalist whose contacts with the upper echelons of the CPD had provided him with so much valuable information. Capone had him killed.

Next, one of his most trusted associates turned informer – not to the police, but to the US Inland Revenue Service. This was vital to the presidential ambition to get Capone, for Hoover, having realized that Capone was clever enough to make sure that none of the crimes he committed could be pinned on him had turned to Andrew Mellon, the Secretary of the Treasury, to get something on him.

Mellon, in turn, looked to an innocuous-seeming, mild-mannered official, Elmer L. Irey, for help. Irey and his team, including Frank Wilson, a US Treasury man whose investigation had already put several gangsters behind bars for tax evasion, set to work on their new job.

They quickly established that Al Capone had never filed a tax return – no crime for anyone whose income was less than $5,000 a year. On the surface, it seemed that it would be easy to prove that a man who in three years had spent $25,000 on furniture, $7,000 on suits and $40,000 on phone calls. But Al Capone had no bank accounts and had been clever enough to put all the trappings of his wealth if not in the names of members of his families then in the name of third parties who could trust implicitly.

The authorities uncovered enough evidence to get Capone sent down for three years at most. But Washington wanted him out of the way for longer than that. Wilson's persistence paid off when he eventually persuaded some of the men on the Capone payroll to talk. By 1931 the US Internal Revenue had enough evidence to charge Al Capone with failure to pay tax on the $1 million

they had proof he had earned between 1925 and 1929. Everyone knew that that was a fraction of the true figure but it was enough to threaten a 30-year sentence.

At first, it seemed that Capone would escape a long sentence. His lawyers reached a deal with the DA's office that if their client pleaded guilty, he would be sentenced to no more that two and a half years. However, this was rejected by federal judge James H. Wilkerson, who had been appointed to hear the case.

Capone withdrew his 'guilty' plea and the case went to court.

On 24 October, Alphonse Capone, still only 31 years old, was sentenced to eleven years in prison and fined $50,000 plus costs of $30,000. It was the harshest sentence ever handed down for tax evasion. Not only that, his few assets and all of his wife's were seized by the government. But as most of the Capone fortune was held in other names, including the company that owned Al's Florida estate, most of his fortune remained in the family.

Capone's lawyers lodged an appeal. When it failed he was taken to Atlanta Federal Penitentiary to serve his sentence. But his fellow inmates were so in awe of him that it soon became obvious to the authorities that this was no punishment, and he was sent to the new prison at Alcatraz, on an island in San Francisco Bay.

Shortly after he had been arrested, Capone had been diagnosed as suffering from syphilis, which he had probably contacted in one of his own brothels. Slowly and insidiously the

The Opera House, symbol of Chicago, towers over the skyline of the city.

disease ran its course. In February 1938 his fellow inmates in Alcatraz were astonished to see the once all-powerful Chicago gangster enter the mess hall in a daze, spittle dripping from his mouth. Tests in the prison hospital confirmed that the disease had entered its final stages his brain was turning into jelly.

Within a few months he was paralyzed and in January 1939 he was released from Alcatraz and after a short spell at the Federal Correctional Institution outside Los Angeles, he was sent to a medical centre in Philadelphia where he was judged to be insane. In November the same year he was released into the care of his family.

During his time in jail, his empire had flourished under the direction of men who never forgave the men who turned against their old leader, to the extent that eleven days before Capone was released, unknown assassins gunned down one of them as he drove home from a ball game.

His old henchmen continued to visit him in Florida, feeding his delusions that he was still in charge of Chicago's gangland, telling him of how successful his old rackets were and how promising the new ones were proving. But they all knew that, in the words of one of them, 'Al is nutty a fruitcake.'

He died on January 25, 1947, after suffering a massive brain haemorrhage. His body was taken back to Chicago where it was buried after a small, quiet ceremony that was a million miles away from the lavish, floral-laden gangsters' funerals of the Roaring Twenties when Al Capone was King of the Windy City

The Genna Family

One Family of the Cosa Nostra who had more right to consider themselves as 'family' than all the others was the Genna gang – six brothers who must count among the most lethal and ruthless gangsters ever to roam the streets of Chicago. They were born in Marsala in Sicily and sailed to the United States in 1910 when their father took a job on the Chicago Railway.

Their mother died when they were little. With their father at work, they grew up wild on the streets of the city, where shootings were a dime a dozen, where bombings were commonplace, where knives flashed as often as the local prostitutes hooked a client and where the Black Hand Gangs demanded money from whoever they felt would pay – or else.

When their father died in 1900, the brothers were taken under the wing of Diamond Joe Esposito, a baker-cum-gangster, who encouraged the boys in their life of crime. After years of fighting street battles, they took to it like fish to water. By the time that Sam, Angelo and Mike Genna were sending Black Hand letters, usually to their fellow Sicilian immigrants, Jim was running a brothel, and Antonio and Peter were pimping for him.

They recruited their soldiers from fellow Sicilian immigrants and, like them, the brothers were deeply religious; so much so that they carried crucifixes in the pockets where they kept their guns; guns that five of them would use at the blink of the eyelids that hooded their dark, Italian eyes. The other one, Tony the Gentleman, was personally opposed to killing: doing it himself, that is. He was more than happy for his brothers to kill; indeed he sat in on family councils of war when the fate of rivals was openly discussed. There, he would ask his murdering brothers why they ran the risk of killing, when they had more than enough men in their ranks to do the dirty work for them.

There was Sam Amatuna who whistled arias from the operas he loved as he took aim and fired. They had in their ranks Guiseppe Nerone, also known as 'The Cavalier', a mathematics graduate who had given up a promising teaching career to join the Gennas' mob. And there was the terrible duo Albert Anselmi and John Scalise who rubbed the bullets they used with garlic, hoping that if a target survived the gunfire, the garlic would induce gangrene into the wounds.

Many Mafiosi considered themselves men of culture. Tony Genna was one of the few who actually lived up to the claim. He loved architecture and could discuss the finer points of Ionic, Doric and Corinthian pillars with experts in the field. He was a noted patron of the opera. And he built tenements for his fellow immigrants in Chicago's Little Italy, although he, unlike his brothers, moved out of the area at the first opportunity and lived in style in a smart downtown hotel, The

Congress, where he occupied a $100-a-day suite with his mistress Gladys Bagwell. Unusually for a gangster's moll, Gladys was the daughter of a Baptist minister who had run away to Chicago where she got a job singing in a bar owned by Johnny Torrio.

In 1919, with Prohibition looming, the Gennas decided to get into the distilling business, and soon families all over Little Italy were producing raw alcohol. The brothers paid their illegal distillers $15 a day, each one producing around 350 gallons a week. It cost them a few cents to process it further before they sold it on for $2 wholesale, giving them a large profit.

At first, they agreed to sell it at that price to John Torrio and Al Capone who controlled the bars, brothels in the city's south and west sides. Within a year they realized how much more they could make if they sold it direct to the final consumer, and established a string of bars in the near west side, which soon became undisputed Genna territory.

Their operations grossed them $350,000 a month. Their expenses were high, around $200,000 a month. But even so, the brothers were soon netting $2 million a year. They spent it on jewels and furs for their wives and girlfriends, whom they wined and dined in the best restaurants and entertained at Chicago's Opera House where they had twelve front-row season tickets every year.

In order to operate without being bothered by the police, gangsters needed the protection of local politicians and the police. The police were easy! At the local Maxwell Street precinct, the brothers had five captains, four hundred uniformed officers and just as many headquarters plain-clothes men on the payroll, as well as countless others in the DA's office. They were paid between $10 and $125 a month depending on how important they were and how long they had been in the brothers' pay.

Once a month, one by one, the bent cops trooped in to the brothers' headquarters on Taylor Street to collect their bribes. It wasn't long before cops from other parts of the city were joining the queue, claiming to be in the Maxwell Street station. To solve the problem, the Maxwell Street boys gave the brothers a list of badge numbers, so that they could tell bona fide bent cops from impostors!

The police helped ensure the Genna brothers' monopoly on illegal distilling was maintained. They gave the boys from Maxwell Street a list of their own stills, and when a non-Genna one was discovered, the police swung into action. Press photographers, tipped off in advance, were on hand to snap the action, so that the good citizens of Chicago could see how hard the Maxwell Street police were fighting crime in their precinct.

The brothers were among the first to break the agreement that Johnny Torrio tried to impose on Chicago's gangs – Mafia, Irish, Poles, wherever – splitting up the city into territories wherein each of them would run their rackets free from interference from the others.

In the ensuing gun battles that must have made the World War One trenches seem like a haven of peace to ex-US servicemen who had seen service in Flanders just a dozen or so years ago, three of the Gennas met their ends.

First to go was Angelo.

After Charlie O'Bannion was murdered in his flower shop late in 1924, the Gennas began to expand their operations in the north side. Angelo, by now head of the *Unione Siciliane*, had married Lucille Spingola, the daughter of a prominent politician, and moved her into a suite in the city's Belmont Hotel, in the heart of O'Bannion territory.

On 25 May he was driving his sporty roadster through the city's iron-grid streets to put a $25,000 deposit on a property he hoped to move into with his new bride. When he became aware that he was being tailed, he put his foot down hard. As he picked up speed he took a corner too fast and skidded into a lamp post with such force that the bonnet crumbled and he was left pinned behind the wheel. There was nothing he could do but watch the car come to a halt beside his and see the windows be wound down. Three of Charlie O'Bannion's men armed with shotgun, revolver and submachine gun leaned out and began to fire. Angelo died almost instantly, his body ripped apart by the assassins' bullets.

Next to go was Mike. After he had identified his brother's body at the city morgue, he telephoned Albert Anselmi and ordered him and John Scalise to help get revenge. What Mike didn't know was that the two gunmen had switched sides and were now on Al Capone's payroll. Capone had learned that the brothers were plotting to have him murdered and had promised the pair that if they eliminated them, he would pay them a fortune.

On 13 June, Mike Genna clambered into a car with Anslemi and Scalise, to search for the trio who had slain his brother. This was a ploy. The two covert Capone men planned to drive to a quiet spot and dispose of Genna in the usual way. But as they drove along the city streets, their car was spotted by a police patrol who, believing the men inside to be armed, gave chase. With Genna at the wheel, the car roared along Western Avenue, when a truck pulled out in front of it. Genna pulled on the wheel. The car leapt onto the pavement and came to a halt when it slammed into a lamp post.

The three gangsters grabbed their guns and leapt out of the car just as the police car screeched to a halt. In the gun battle that followed one policeman was killed and two were injured. With one of the surviving policemen hot on their tail, the three mobsters turned and ran, Mike Genna trailing the other two who spotted an open clothes shop and hid inside it. As he ran, Genna turned and fired at the pursuing policeman who returned his fire, hitting the Mafia man in the leg. He dived through the window of a basement, but he was cornered.

The police bullet had severed an artery. But Mike Genna was not one to give up easily. When he was being taken on stretcher into the ambulance that the police summoned, he kicked one of the ambulance men, catching him in the jaw and knocking

him out cold. 'Take that, you son of a bitch,' he roared.

He died before surgeons could operate, never knowing that the two men he had been with had been planning to kill him.

To say that Tony 'The Gentlemen' and his three remaining brothers were starting to feel the heat is something of an understatement. Tony barricaded himself in his hotel suite, sending Gladys out to buy whatever room service couldn't supply. While he was holed up, his chief lieutenant, Guiseppe 'The Cavalier' Nerone phoned him, telling him that Capone had been behind the murders. When he heard tha, Tony knew he had to get out of town.

Nerone told him to wait a day or two so they could make plans. He said that while they were out of town, he would build up the gang to the point where it could take Capone out and then the four Genna boys could come back, the city at their feet.

Genna agreed to meet Nerone to talk things through. On 8 July, he drove from his hotel to the rendezvous, a grocery store, which was a front for a Genna illegal still. When he spotted Nerone lurking in the doorway, he wound down the window to check that the coast was clear before getting out and approaching his henchman.

Nerone offered a handshake. Genna took it. But as the two men stood there, another pair (probably Anselmi and Scalise) darted out of a doorway and shot Tony in the back. Nerone had taken Capone's dollar.

Capone's three thugs ran to a waiting car and drove off, leaving

Tony Genna, blood running from the gunshot wounds, slumped on the pavement, for dead.

Unfortunately they were wrong, Genna was rushed to hospital where Gladys, her cheeks streaked by mascara, sat by his bedside, willing him to live. 'Who shot you, Tony?' she asked.

'The Cavalier,' he rasped.

They were his last words.

The police misheard the name, and by the time they realised it was Guiseppe Nerone they should have been looking for, he was dead, shot in the barber's chair where he was being shaved.

Tony Genna's funeral was a lavish affair. The coffin alone cost $10,000. More than twice that amount's worth of flowers adorned the grave, which was a few yards away from Charlie O'Bannion's. As a cynical policeman observed, 'When judgement day comes and these graves are open, there'll be hell to pay.'

The Gennas were finished. Jim, Peter and Sam fled Chicago and headed for the land of their birth. Back in Chicago, Capone ordered that any members of the Genna gang who refused to work on his team be wiped out. When one of them was tracked down, he knelt, hands clasped in prayer, begging for his life. Capone's gunmen shot off his hands before firing a bullet into his brain. Another was hacked to death, his body parts scattered on a Chicago rubbish dump. In 1930, five years after the order had gone out, the last of the Genna gang, Felipe Gnolfo, was tracked down and dealt with in the usual cold-blooded way.

Meanwhile, back in Sicily, Jim couldn't turn his back on crime. He was put behind bars for stealing the jewels that adorned the Madonna di Trapani. Some say that he ensured that he would be caught and sent to jail where he would be safe from Al Capone's far-reaching tentacles. While their brother was in jail, Sam and Peter sought the safety of the woods of southern Sicily where they knew the local Mafia would protect them,

Years later, having renounced their lives of crime, the three surviving Genna brothers returned to Chicago, no longer in thrall to the gangs that had ruled the city during Prohibition. They set themselves up in business importing cheese and olive oil from Sicily and, unlike their brothers, died in obscurity, but peacefully, a fate denied their three brothers who died as bloodily as they had lived.

Vito Genovese

Among the hundreds of Italian immigrants to the United States who poured down the gangplank of the *SS Taormina* when she docked in New York in May 1923 was fifteen-year-old Vito Genovese. There was little to suggest that the fresh-faced youth would become one of the most murderous, villainous and ruthless gangsters in the history of the Mafia.

He headed for the Lower East Side and had soon fallen into a life of crime, preying on small shopkeepers and selling strong-arm protection to pushcart peddlers. Two years after his arrival in the States, Genovese met Lucky Luciano and joined his gang.

Vito Genovese, one-time 'boss of bosses' in New York, who would die
of a heart attack two years into a fifteen-year sentence in a Federal penitentiary.

Lucky Luciano: one-time partner of Vito Genovese, the two men would end up deadly rivals.

The two took up armed robbery and burglary, but a few months after the meeting, while on his way to a rendezvous with Luciano, Vito was arrested and sentenced to sixty days in the workhouse for carrying a gun. Despite Luciano's promises to get him out, Vito served his full term. Even so, when he was released he teamed up with Luciano again and within a year the two were leading members of 'Little Augie' Orgen's gang.

At first they concentrated on establishing a chain of brothels in Brooklyn and Manhattan and, when Prohibition came in, made fortunes out of bootlegging. But they soon realized that there was something else that many New Yorkers wanted even more than booze, and something that was even more profitable than selling hooch: narcotics.

In the 1920s, drug peddling was considered as an 'unclean' trade by Mafia bosses. But there was one crime overlord in Manhattan who was interesting in expanding into narcotics – the Jewish gambler and rackets-master Arnold Rothstein. It was Rothstein who financed the smuggling of drugs into New York, through Luciano's and Genovese's boss 'Little Augie' Orgen, who in turn handed the drugs traffic to his two trusty lieutenants.

In 1925, Luciano and Genovese switched their loyalties to Joe 'The Boss' Masseria, Mafia chief in New York from 1920 to 1931, when he was assassinated in a classic gangland set-up organized by none other than Lucky Luciano.

But long before that, Genovese used his new boss's contacts to establish an Italian food importing company, narcotics being the bulk of what the company imported.

During the Roaring Twenties, Genovese is said to have killed at least six men personally and ordered the deaths of many more than that number. In the 1930s he played a prominent part in the internecine Castellammare Wars which broke out when Salvatore Maranzano declared that only men from that area in Italy were entitled to run rackets in New York. This was the war that saw the control of the US Mafia pass from Italian-born mobsters to native-born gangsters.

Despite his reputation as one of the most vicious criminals on the New York scene, Vito Genovese was a family man at heart, though even there violence was never far away. Three years after his first wife died in 1929, he met Anna Petillo, who was to give him a son and a daughter. But when they met, Anna was married to a man called Gerard Vernotico. Two weeks after Genovese met Anna, Vernotico was found strangled in a doorway, beside the body of another man who had been shot . . .

Business flourished throughout the 1930s, Luciano concentrating on expanding their prostitution empire coast to coast, and Genovese running the narcotics trafficking. But in 1937 one of Genovese's gunmen, Ernie 'The Hawk' Rupolo 'sang' to Thomas E Dewey, the New York district attorney who had vowed to rid New York of its racketeers, about Genovese's involvement in the murder of Ferdinand 'The Shadow' Boccia. Vito didn't hang around

Salvatore Moretti (fore), on trial
for attempting to bribe & threaten, 1951.

waiting to be hauled in. He was on the first boat to Italy.

A careful man who often stayed up late into the night plotting the moves that would keep him one step ahead in the rackets he ran, Genovese had planned for just such a contingency. He had more than $2 million deposited in Italian and Swiss banks, and a fleet of limousines and a retinue of servants were waiting for him.

Within a few months of arriving in Naples, Vito Genovese was running the Mafia-Camorro drug trafficking operations, establishing a distribution system that started in the Middle East and ended on the streets of major US cities, via Italy and Sicily. And despite Mussolini's campaign to destroy the Mafia, Genovese ingratiated himself to Il Duce through his connection with the Italian leader's foreign minister and son-in-law Count Galeazzo Ciano, whose expensive habit Genovese was only too happy to supply! And just to make sure that he stayed in Mussolini's good books, he arranged the assassination in New York of one of Il Duce's most bitter enemies, newspaper editor Carlo Tresca.

When the Americans landed in Italy in 1944, Genovese, who had been reported killed in an air raid, emerged from the grave and offered himself as a translator to the US Intelligence Service. Among the information that he gave them was the names of everyone involved in black marketeering in Naples and the rest of southern Italy. When they were safely behind bars, Genovese stepped into their shoes, but when the Americans found out not only that he had taken over the black market rackets but that he was wanted for murder in New York he was shipped back to the States.

He however was soon back in action, as all the men who could have given evidence against him were silenced in one way or another: even from his prison cell, Genovese had seen to that. At the end of his trial, the judge said, 'If there was a shred of corroborative evidence against you, you would have been condemned to the electric chair.' He went on to suggest that Genovese had terrorised witnesses, had them kidnapped and murdered. But as there was no evidence, he had no alternative other than to release him.

Vito, believing himself to be above the law, now decided it was time to put his master plan into operation: a plan to gain control of Lucky Luciano's Family, Luciano having been deported to Italy, and with it the dominant role in the US Mafia. There were several obstacles in his way. Luciano still exercised considerable control from across the Atlantic, and the acting head of the Family, Frank Costello, was not going to go easily.

Genovese knew that to achieve his ambition was going to take time and money. The money he got from setting up a secret narcotics racket. The time he bought by paying lip service to Luciano and Costello, and to Meyer Lansky, the Jewish mobster who was a close ally of the Luciano Family.

The first victim of Genovese's ambition was New Jersey Mafia boss Willie Moretti. He was slain in 1951. Next to go was Costello's closest ally Steven Franse in 1953. In May 1957,

an attempt on Costello's life failed but it was enough for him to retire and for Genovese to take over control of the Luciano empire. Genovese was not one to take risks and five months later, Luciano's top exterminator Albert Anastasia was shot while having his hair cut in the barber shop in New York's Park Sheraton Hotel.

Shortly after Anastasia's murder, Genovese and other Mafia leaders summoned more than a hundred top mobsters to Joseph Barbara's estate in Apalachin, in upstate New York, a meeting where Vito Genovese expected to be anointed boss of bosses. But the event was a set-up by Costello, Luciano and Meyer Lansky who, it is said, tipped off the police

Meyer Lansky, Jewish money-launderer and close associate of Lucky Luciano.

who raided the house. And so, rather than being hailed by the nation's criminal bosses, Genovese took the blame for the fiasco. It was also as a direct result of this that the American public, who had come to believe that American gangsters now only existed in the movies, knew they were alive, kicking and responsible for much of the crime in the US.

Even so, Vito Genovese was now the dominant Mafia man in New York. But Frank Costello, Lucky Luciano and Meyer Lansky were to have their revenge. They arranged for a huge amount of drugs to be smuggled into the US and then contrived to lay the blame at Genovese's door. Acting on information supplied by a small time Puerto Rican drug pusher, who was paid $400,000 by the conspirators, Genovese and twenty-four of his men were arrested.

This time there was no escape for Vito Genovese. In 1959 he was sentenced to fifteen years in prison. Even from his cell he continued to exercise his considerable muscle, sending his gunmen to settle old scores. He died, ten years into his sentence, in 1964; two years after Lucky Luciano had died of a heart attack in Naples. Frank Costello died in bed in February 1973. Meyer Lansky outlived them all. Although his later years were dogged by ill health, he lived until 1983 when he died aged eighty-one.

Salvatore Maranzano – The boss of the bosses

Salvatore Maranzano was born in Sicily in 1868 and came to the US from his home town of Castellammare del Golfo around 1918 (the exact date is uncertain). Had the immigration authorities who welcomed him to the States at Ellis Island realized what he would become, they would have sent put him on the first eastbound ship back across the Atlantic! For Maranzano was the founder of the modern US Mafia and became the one and only 'boss of bosses.'

He had been educated in a seminary and his parents had wanted him to become a priest. But Salvatore had other ideas. He was a Mafia man, a follower of Don Vito Cascio Ferro – the most powerful Mafia leader in Sicily. The Don had visited the US and had seen the opportunities the country could afford the Mafia. He saw himself as the head of the organization – *capo de tutti capi* or boss of all bosses.

It was Ferro who sent Maranzano to the States, to start organizing the American crime families, even non-Italian ones, into one big 'Family'. Unfortunately before Ferro could sail to the States to claim his place at the head of the table, he was arrested by the Fascists and sent to prison for the rest of his life.

Maranzano surrounded himself with Sicilians, men like Joseph Prophecy, Joe Nonagon and Stefano Magazine and other recently-arrived immigrants who resented the way that US-born gangsters looked down on them.

With Ferro in jail, Maranzano took over the mantle of would-be capo de tutti capi, head of a criminal organization all of whose members owed him absolute allegiance. But standing in his way were mobsters who were too ensconced in the old ways to listen to him. Maranzano referred to these mobsters as 'Moustache Petes' and set about converting them to his way of seeing things.

At first he played kept a relatively low profile, dabbling in Manhattan's bootlegging and gambling rackets. But as the 1920s roared along, more and more immigrant Italians were recruited to the Maranzano mob and by 1928 he was becoming so powerful that the foremost Mafia boss in New York, Guiseppe Masseria or 'Joe the Boss', started to realize that Maranzano was a threat to his operations.

For his part, the Sicilian regarded Masseria as one of the Moustache Petes he loathed so much and when the 'Joe the Boss' began to move in on the rackets that Maranzano's henchmen were running in Brooklyn, he decided to act. He knew that other Mafia mobs on New York resented the tributes that Masseria demanded of them and started to cultivate this resentment. He promised them that in return for their allegiance he would give them a much fairer share of their proceeds of their crimes. Among the men he tried to lure from Masseria's mob was Lucky Luciano who was one of 'the Boss's' most trusted lieutenants – but Luciano had plans of his own and stayed loyal to Masseria.

By the end of 1928, Masseria had had enough and declared war, confident that with more guns at his command he would soon cut the upstart Sicilian down to size. For two years the Castellammare War raged with more than fifty men from both sides being shot. The exact number was impossible for the police to establish. The NYPD had little way of knowing if a bullet-smashed body found in back alley had been a Masseria mobster or one of Maranzano's men, or just another gangster caught in the crossfire of the war between other bootlegging gangs that raging all over the underworld.

As the war blazed, a new factor came into play. Lucky Luciano, still ostensibly one of Masseria's most trusted lieutenants, had been spending time and effort cultivating young gangsters on both sides, intending eventually to ally the Italian mobsters from both gangs with Jewish criminals into a syndicate that would make not just for a bigger cake but also a large slice for all involved. Key to his plan was Meyer Lansky, one of the great criminal minds of the twentieth century. All but a few of the Jewish gangs with whom he had contact liked the idea of forming a national crime syndicate in alliance with the Mafia.

New York mobsters were impressed with Luciano, whose tentacles stretched high up into the NYPD and into the upper reaches of the political world. And Luciano, with his contacts in both Maranzano's and The Boss's organizations, knew what the two were up to.

Lansky and Luciano decided to play a waiting game, letting the two gangs slug and shoot it out on the streets of New York and inevitably weakening each other until one perished and one was seemingly victorious. Then, and only then, would Luciano and Meyer strike.

But as the months passed, Masseria and Maranzano's guns were still blazing, with the Sicilian giving better than he was getting. In 1931, fearful that Maranzano's seemingly impending victory would attract so many supporters that he would be in an unassailable position, Luciano decided to speed the game up. He inveigled Masseria to lunch in a Coney Island diner on April 15, luring him there with the promise of a high-stake poker game after the meal. As the others in the restaurant gradually drifted off, the cards were shuffled and dealt and the game got underway. After a hand or two, Luciano excused himself and made for the men's room. While he was there, some of his men including Albert Anastasia, 'Bugsy' Siegel and Joe Adonis burst into the restaurant, guns ablaze. By the time Luciano strolled out of the men's room. Masseria was dead, hit by six bullets and lying face down in a pool of his own blood.

Back on Manhattan, Luciano declared the war over. A seemingly grateful Maranzano made Luciano his chief. Later, he rented a large hall on Washington Street in the Bronx and called a meeting of the city's top mobsters. Five hundred of the old rivals who a few months before had been shooting at each other now rubbed shoulders.

According to Joe Valachi, one of the mobsters present and who thirty-

one years later was to testify before the Congressional subcommittee into the Mafia, Maranzano sat on a throne beneath a huge cross and called for silence. He accused 'Joe the Boss' of having started the Castellammare War and said that now they were over things would be different. He announced that he was the capo de tutti capi and that new Families were to be established. Each Family was to have its own boss and an under-boss or chief lieutenant. Under him would be junior lieutenants or *caporegimes*. As he rambled on in grandiose fashion, he said the other members were to be the foot soldiers, each of whom was to be assigned to a lieutenant.

Valachi said that during his speech Maranzano used the expression Cosa Nostra ('This thing of ours') – the first time he had heard it. The FBI claim that it was they who originated the expression. It doesn't matter who first coined the phrase. What is relevant is that, as we said in the Introduction, the words refer to the US Mafia and were never meant to apply to their Sicilian cousins.

Maranzano rambled on and on, outlining the rules. First, loyalty was absolute: total obedience was demanded at all levels. The capo de tutti capi's word was law right down the line. All breaches were punishable by death. Any Cosa Nostra member who had sex with another member's wife would be shot. The same fate awaited anyone who publicized the Mafia initiation rites, anyone who discussed Mafia business with a non-member, even a wife, and anyone who sought vengeance for the events of the War. 'Even if your own brother was killed, don't try to find out who did it or get even. If you do, you will pay with your life.'

Listening to all this were Luciano and one of his most important allies, Vito Genovese, They both liked the idea of the family structure but they both felt that having rid gangland of one ruthless leader, they had replaced them with another. And, looking around him, Luciano realized that his endgame – his plan for the Italian-Jewish alliance – would be difficult to put into operation with Maranzano able to call the shots of the five hundred men in the hall, and no doubt countless others hanging out in the pool-halls and brothels of the city. They decided to eliminate the Sicilian.

But Maranzano was no fool. He knew that Luciano had been negotiating terms with Meyer Lansky to create his own power base. He also knew that his fellow Sicilian com-manded the loyalty of several of the top men in the new Cosa Nostra. He decided that Luciano, Vito Genovese, Frank Costello, Joseph Adonis, Salvatore Moretti, Dutch Schultz, and, although not a Mafia member, Al Capone, who was now in Chicago, all posed strong enough threats to his security that they should die.

He knew that eliminating the men on his death list would be no easy task. He devised a plan, hoping to have some of them killed before the other realized who was behind it and another all-out war erupted. He also decided to use non-Italian hit men so that he could hold his hands up in innocent horror. The first man he

recruited was the gloriously named 'Mad Dog' Coll, a young Irish killer. He told Coll to come to his Park Avenue office at a date and time when he would arrange for the first two victims – Luciano and Genovese – to be there. After the pair had been shot, Coll was to 'lose' the bodies and move on to the next on the list before they realized what was afoot. The Irishman was given a down payment of $25,000 with the promise of the same again after the pair had been assassinated.

But Luciano got wind of what was going on and hatched a plot of his own. He was tipped off by one of his men that he and Genovese were to be summoned to Maranzano's office where they were to be gunned down. The call came through on September 10, 1931. As soon as he got it, Luciano put his own plan into operation. A few minutes before he and Vito Genovese were scheduled to arrive, one of Maranzano's henchmen, Tommy Lushes, sauntered into his office. Maranzano had no idea that 'Three Fingers' Lushes had switched loyalties and was now in Lucky Luciano's pocket.

Just after he went in to see Maranzano, four policemen burst in, flashing their ID badges and demanding to question the Sicilian. But they were no NY cops. Rather, they were four Jewish hitmen that Luciano had borrowed from Meyer Lansky, knowing that Maranzano would not recognize them. He also knew that the four men would not recognize Maranzano, but that they knew 'Three Fingers', which is why he was present. He had been told to stand close to Maranzano and away from any bodyguards so that the Jewish gunmen would know whom to shoot at.

The 'cops' showed their badges to Giraloma Santucci, who screened Maranzano's visitors. He called Maranzano from his office and when he emerged with 'Three Fingers' at his side, the 'cops' drew their guns. But before they could pull the triggers, one of the men drew a knife and went for the self-proclaimed capo de tutti capi. Maranzano fended him off as best he could, but was stabbed six times. With blood gushing from the wounds, he somehow summoned the strength to dive at the

The liquor flows in an illegal speakeasy, Chicago, 1925.

others. But they pointed their guns at the bleeding Sicilian and emptied the chambers into him.

They then turned their attention on Maranzano. One of them men pulled out a knife and stabbed him to death. They had no orders regarding the bodyguards, and as the hit men ran from the office and headed for the emergency stairs, the terrified henchmen were just behind them. On the way down one of them bumped into 'Mad Dog' Coll, on his way to keep his own appointment. When he found out what had been going on, the Irishman turned and joined the bodyguards on the way out. According to one of them Coll, $25,000 better off and with no one to shoot, whistled as he went. (He didn't whistle for long. Five months later, he was shot down in a hail of gunfire when making a telephone call from a phone booth in a drug store on West 23rd Street.)

By the time the real New York police arrived on the scene all they found was Maranzano's still-warm body. Everyone else had fled. By the time the police were back at their headquarters reports were coming in from other parts of the country of other gangland assassinations. Within a day or two, forty of Maranzano's associates had been killed. Lucky Luciano had silenced all the Maranzano opposition in one brilliantly planned coup. Among the dead were James Marino, Sam Monaco and Louis Rosso who, although they had claimed to have switched sides to Luciano, were suspected of still being loyal to the dead Sicilian. They were tortured, murdered and thrown into the river. Their mutilated bodies were found floating in Newark Bay to the south of Manhattan a few days after Maranzano's assassination.

The only capo de tutti capi in the history of the American Mafia was dead, and with him went the reign of the immigrant Italians, the Moustache Petes, whom Maranzano had despised but of which he was one, to the American mobs. From now on, it was the American Mafia not the Sicilian one that ruled the roost in the United States. But the Maranzano legacy lived on. Lucky Luciano retained the family structure the Sicilian had ranted on about in the hall on Washington Street a few months before he was assassinated – the one and only boss of the bosses.

John Torrio

Apart from being among the most notorious gangsters in US history, apart from being one of the, perhaps *the* brains behind the Commission (the Mafia board of directors which was established to settle inter-family disputes), John Torrio has another claim to fame. He taught Al Capone everything he knew.

John Torrio was born in Osara in Italy in 1882. His father worked in the vineyards, scrimping and saving to get the money together to emigrate to the States. By the time Johnny was two, his father had enough for the passage to New York, but he never lived to see the city. He died a few weeks before he and his wife were due to sail.

Torrio claimed that his mother was so poor that the only clothes he had when he arrived in New York was the tattered girl's dress he was wearing when he tottered down the gangplank, a piece of paper bearing his name pinned to its bodice. (This is probably true. In the early years of the twentieth century it was common

practice for boys to be dressed as girls until they went to school.)

Johnny's mother, Maria Carlucci, got a job as a seamstress in the Italian ghetto on the Lower East Side where she met and later married Salvatore Caputo, who ran a grocer's shop in the area. He also ran an illegal bar behind the shop where Johnny later worked mopping the floor, no doubt listening to the tales the exclusively Italian and Sicilian clientele told about their lives of petty crime.

Like so many kids on the Lower East Side block, he grew up on the street, and joined the James Street Gang where he was initiated into the life of crime that he was to follow. Johnny was a loner when it came to the robberies he committed, reasoning that if he worked on his own, no one could squeal on him.

But when it came to fighting for the gang, 'Terrible Johnny' was in there with the best of them. He may have been small, but he packed a powerful punch and could wield a knife as well as any man. He was a mean, calculating little fighter, something that qualified him to get a job as bouncer in a bar called Nigger Mick's on the Bowery's Pell Street. There, he probably met one of the singing waiters who got his first job there – a Jewish kid who became famous as Irving Berlin.

By the time he was 22 he had made enough to start a business. Calling himself JT McCarthy, the diminutive Italian opened a bar on the corner of James and Walker Streets near the Brooklyn navy yards. As well as the ground-floor bar, he also rented the upper rooms and the building next door and set up twenty or so prostitutes in business. A business like that needed protection, not just from rival gangsters but from the seamen who frequented it. John Torrio hired a band of the meanest, toughest strong-arm men in New York, most of the Italian immigrants like himself, or the American-born children of Italian immigrants.

Soon bar owning and brothel keeping weren't enough for the ambitious young man. He moved into gambling, hijacking and the narcotics business. His growing businesses soon came to the attention of Paul Kelly (aka Paulo Vaccarelli), then the most powerful of the New York gang overlords. He persuaded the enterprising young man to join him in the rackets he ran all over Manhattan, and by 1905 he had risen to be Kelly's number one lieutenant.

As well as running Kelly's brothels, Torrio also acted as tutor to a gang of willing young kids, initiating them into the art of petty robberies, pickpocketing and other street crimes. Torrio 'bought' whatever they stole for a fraction of what it was worth, then selling it for a handsome profit.

If Johnny Torrio was Fagin then one of the kids he influenced was his Artful Dodger – Al Capone. The young thug so impressed Capone that he hired him as strong-arm protection at his. The two became so close that Capone later said that he looked on Johnny Torrio as a father.

In 1909, Torrio received a summons from 'Big Jim' Colosimo, who was married to his aunt, Victoria Moresco. 'Big Jim' and Victoria were

an ideal match: she was a brothel keeper and he was one of the biggest whoremasters in Chicago. The biggest fly in his ointment was the Black Hand who were threatening to beat up his prostitutes and their clients and burn his gambling dens and saloons unless they were given a cut of the profits – $50,000 a week. Colosimo wanted them off his back, and from what he knew about his wife's nephew, he was just the man for the job.

Shortly after he arrived in Chicago, Torrio took over The Saratoga, Colosimo's biggest brothel and set himself up as its 'madam'. Not long afterwards he set up a meeting with three of the top Black Handers who he knew were acting under orders from their boss, 'Sunny Jim' Cosamano, promising to bring with him the first instalment of the money they were demanding.

In fact, he took with him the cream of Colosimo's gunmen and instead of giving the Black Handers the money, they gave the extortionists the bullets in their guns; in their heads, chests and limbs. That done, Torrio sent word to 'Sunny Jim' that one more Black Hand threat to his uncle, and he, Torrio, would personally kill Cosamano. As soon as he received the message, the Black Hand boss announced he was retiring.

From then on, Johnny Torrio made Chicago the scene of his activities. He sold his share in the Harvard Inn, his New York quarters to Frankie Yale, a gangster who, in 1927, gained the distinction of being the first New York racketeer to be killed by machine-gun fire.

Torrio and his wife, Anna, rented an apartment in Chicago's expensive south side, and while Anna established herself on the city's social scene, her husband went to work for his uncle. His first job was to make sure that Colosimo's collectors were paid precisely what was due to their boss from the various rackets he controlled. Colosimo was so impressed with his nephew-by-marriage's efficiency that he eventually more or less handed it over to him.

From his headquarters, the Four Deuces, Torrio expanded the business, adding countless millions to his uncle's already bulging coffers, not to mention his own.

Towards the end of 1919, Johnny Torrio summoned Capone to Chicago. He told his uncle that he needed the young New York mobster to protect him and help him run the brothels. In fact, knowing that Prohibition was about to be imposed and realizing the opportunities this would present, he wanted Al to organize that side of the business

'Big Jim' Colosimo wasn't interested in bootlegging. He was fabulously rich and by now notoriously lazy. Torrio decided he had to go. He couldn't do it. He didn't want Al Capone, by now his number one lieutenant, to get involved. There was only one man for the job – Frankie Yale.

In May 1920, 'Big Jim' was approached by a contact in the liquor business who promised him a large consignment of bonded alcohol that would keep his bars going until Prohibition, something Colosimo

believed would last only a few months, ended.

The bar was still closed when 'Big Jim' arrived to take delivery of the liquor. As someone who always dealt in cash, he had $10,000 dollars in his billfolds, and never one to try to hide his wealth, his tiepin, rings, cufflinks and belt buckle glittered with $50,000 worth of diamonds. A few of his employees had arrived for work by the time Colosimo arrived at the bar. Most of them were in the back, setting up the tables. 'Big Jim' waited in the foyer for the truck carrying the booze. As he stood there, gazing out of the small window in the door, Yale crept up behind him, pressed the barrel of a .38 calibre revolver to his head and pulled the trigger. Colosimo slumped to the floor, bits of his brains trickling down the glass window.

His uncle dead, Johnny Torrio took over the entire operation. He had plans, not only for 'Big Jim's' gang – he had plans for all the gangs in Chicago, wanting to bring them all under one umbrella organization with each one running rackets in their own, clearly defined territory. He called a meeting of all the gangs in Chicago – the Italian ones (most of whom, like his own, had Mafia connections), the Irish ones that controlled the city's north side, the Poles who ran things in the south of the city and the other, smaller, ones that ran various scams and rackets, bars and brothels, in other parts of the city and who paid protection money to their more powerful brothers in crime.

He told them that the city's crime cake was large enough for everyone to have a decent slice, and that if they could come to some sort of agreement as to who did what, who controlled which scams, what parts of the city belonged to which gang, then they could all make millions and what's more, live long enough to enjoy their wealth. For despite the fact that he was a master criminal, Johnny Torrio was a family man. He dressed expensively and, unlike many of his contemporaries, conservatively. And he loved nothing more than a night at the opera, and if his good friend Enrico Caruso was singing, then so much the better.

Most of his fellow gang leaders were persuaded by Torrio's logic – and his threats. Especially his threats, Some said they were in, but weren't. Some were in for a short time, but then greed and the other usual suspects took over, and it wasn't long before the streets of Chicago were as mean as they ever had been.

First to renege was the south side Irish mob – the O'Donnell Gang. It took Torrio and Capone two years from 1923 to 1925 to blast them off the street. Among the gunmen who helped shoot at least a dozen Irishmen was Sam 'Golf Bag' Harris who earned his nickname by carrying his shotgun in a golf bag. By 1925 Spike O'Donnell had had enough and quit the game.

Torrio, by now, ran a vast, illegal brewing industry. Much of his beer was brewed in officially closed federal breweries that kept going clandestinely for him. He owned a string of breweries across the state line in Indiana. Torrio beer cost at most $5 a barrel to make. He sold it,

mainly through two of the gangs he controlled, for $45 a barrel. He sold hundreds of thousands of barrels a week. And illegal brewing was only one of his rackets. He imported liquor, ran gambling dens, brothels and the usual protection scams.

New York's Bowery district, home territory of Johnny Torrio, mentor to Al Capone.

He was still open to new opportunities but when Charlie O'Bannion, part-time florist and big-time gangster, offered to sell him the hugely profitable Seiben Brewery for half a million dollars, he was at first suspicious. It was only when O'Bannion claimed that he wanted to give up his rackets and enjoy his retirement with his family that Torrio, a family man himself, agreed.

A week after the deal was done and the money had been handed over, federal agents raided the brewery and confiscated all the equipment. When Torrio found out that O'Bannion had been tipped off in advance about the deal and suckered him into taking the loss he was furious. According to his henchmen he stormed around his office, brandishing a gun, screaming vengeance on the Irish mobster.

In the event, it wasn't Johnny Torrio's gun that fired the fatal bullet that sent Charlie O'Bannion sprawling in his flower shop a few days later. It belonged to one of two of Torrio's hitmen – Albert Anselmi or John Scalise. The killing sparked the biggest, bloodiest gang war in Chicago's history. Torrio knew that he was the most obvious target for a revenge killing.

Ten weeks after the O'Bannion slaying, O'Bannion's men tried to take their revenge. As Torrio and his wife made their way from their chauffeur-driven limousine to their apartment building, a black Cadillac pulled up across the road. Two of O'Bannion's men jumped out, aimed their automatics at Torrio and pulled the trigger. As he slumped the ground, one of the men, 'Bugs' Moran, ran across the road and pushed his gun into the fallen, but still conscious Torrio's head and said, This is for Deanie, you dago bastard,' and pulled the trigger. But it was empty. Before he could reload it, the wail of sirens announced that the police were on their way, and Moran darted back to the waiting car, which roared off.

Torrio was rushed to hospital where Al Capone and thirty of his men stood guard until he was released. Shortly afterwards he was sentenced to nine months' imprisonment in Waukegan Country Jail for bootlegging. Bullet-proof windows were fitted to his cell, which was made comfortable on the orders of the warder, who it was claimed was on the Torrio payroll.

During his time in jail, Johnny Torrio came to a big decision. He had risen from the slums of New York to be one of the top men on the Chicago crime scene. He had accumulated a fortune of $75 million, most of it safely stashed away in New York and European banks. He had a doting wife (but no children). His dream of setting up a syndicate of Chicago criminals was not going to happen – at least not in the immediate future. And he knew that there were men in the O'Bannion gang who wouldn't rest until he was dead. He summoned Al Capone and his lawyers to his prison. When the twenty-five-year-old hoodlum arrived, he was stunned to hear that the man he had come to regard as his father was going to retire. Not only that, he was handing over his empire to Capone.

Not long afterwards, a motorcade fit for the President escorted Johnny and Anne Torrio from their south side apartment to the station where they boarded the famous *Twentieth Century* train that took them to New York. From there, they headed for the Florida sunshine and retirement. But when they found out that O'Bannion's men were hot on their trail, they sailed to Naples where they lived for two years. They would have stayed longer, but when Benito Mussolini started his campaign against the Mafia, Torrio decided it was time to go back to the States.

He settled in New York, surrounded by guards. There he invested in real estate and along with Lucky Luciano, Meyer Lansky and some other old associates, established a business distributing liquor down the east coast from New York to Florida. The venture added to the millions he already had, and even more money flowed in when Prohibition ended. And the business, now legal, boomed. He still dreamed of establishing a national criminal syndicate and was instrumental in setting up the Mafia Commission, a sort of mobsters' parliament that settled inter-gang disputes and approved take-overs (or punished those behind the ones the Commission were against).

But in April 1936 he was arrested for tax evasion. Bail was set at $100,000. A few hours later his ever-loyal wife arrived at the station where he was being held and handed over a package wrapped in newspaper. Inside were one hundred brand new $1,000 bills. After a long trial, and several appeals, in 1939, Johnny Torrio was back in jail again, this time in the Leavenworth Federal Penitentiary, for two-and-a-half years.

After his release in 1941, he spent most of his days walking in the park, or staying in his apartment, venturing out each day, in classic gangster fashion, to be shaved, and in classic gangster fashion with the chair facing the door so he could see who was coming in. He and Anna occasionally dined out in restaurants, sometimes alone, sometimes with friends. He stayed aloof from the gangs that were fighting it out on the streets of New York. He probably offered advice to old comrades, and he was still influential in the Commission, which met every five years. But he was never actively involved in gangland rackets again. (Or, if he was, the men he did business with never talked about it.) He wanted to die, peacefully, in bed.

As it happened, he didn't. On 16 April, 1957, aged seventy-five, he started his day as he usually did – calling at his local barber shop for a shave. No sooner had the hot towels been placed round his neck than he slumped in the chair, the victim of a massive heart attack. He died a few hours later, Anna at his side, in New York's Cumberland Hospital.

His funeral was a far cry from the lavish ones he had attended in his heyday in Chicago when he had controlled a $50-million-a-year crime empire. Less than twenty people stood round the grave in Greenwood Cemetery to pay their last respects to Johnny Torrio, the man who, in his own words, had owned the Chicago police. Anna Torrio made no announcement about his death: it was not until three weeks after his funeral that the press found out he was dead.

THE YAKUZA

WHAT the Mafia is to Sicily, the Cosa Nostra to the United States and the Triads to China, the Yakuza is to Japan. With a legacy stretching almost four centuries to the street peddlers and gamblers of the Samurai era, the Yakuza is one of the oldest and most entrenched of all the criminal organizations in the world.

In common with the Mafia and the others, there is no one gang called 'Yakuza'. It is an association of gangs, from various parts of the country with their own leaders and own areas of expertise, who have forged alliances with one another to form a criminal network that is responsible for most of Japan's organized crime and whose influence goes to the heart of Japanese society.

During the Second World War, they controlled the black market in Japan, and in the War's aftermath they infiltrated their way not just into a variety of shady businesses, but into the Japanese government itself. And during the 1970s and 1980s, Yakuza members made the quantum leap from running local gangs into the boardrooms of multi-national companies. They used the modest inroads they had made into the sleazy world of the Southeast Asian sex trade as a springboard for criminal operations around the world. And like their Mafia counterparts in the United States, realizing that legitimate operations could be just as lucrative as illegal ones, they began investing the proceeds of their nefarious activities in properly established businesses. One of the results of this was to make the grey area between the legal activities of the criminal and the criminal activities of the legitimate greyer than ever before. In 1999, for example, Japanese police uncovered the fact that a Yakuza-affiliated boss was the second-largest individual investor in Japanese airlines!

The former head of the Japan's National Police Agency's organized-crime division, Raisuke Miyawaki, claims that virtually all facets of Japanese society are squeezed by the Yakuza's grip. He goes as far as to blame unrecoverable Yakuza loans and shady, but legal, deals as being among the main causes of the country's recent woes. These have seen Japan's economy stagnate for years and its once mighty stock exchange fall from the giddy peaks it reached in the late 1970s to the doldrums in which it languishes today.

They are into politics. Like their Mafia counterparts in Sicily, Yakuza members openly run for political office and, as Miyawaki said, 'What they don't win, they buy!', citing as an example Shin Kanemaru. He was the man who, in 1992 when he was the most powerful politician in Japan's dominant political party, took a Yakuza pay-off – four million dollars worth of Japanese yen, in 10,000 yen notes – and used a shopping trolley to have them taken to his car!

They are into the leisure industry, running golf courses (a hugely expensive and widely popular sport in Japan) and holiday resorts.

They are into pornography, selling anything from soiled underwear to videos of the most graphic nature.

They are into money-laundering in a big way; allegations involving one of the United States largest airline manufacturers and a $12.6 million payment to a leading Yakuza boss as a kickback for his help in negotiating a $320 million dollar contract with the Japanese government have never been satisfactory explained.

They are into contract killings; a favourite method being 'pavement hijacking' whereby the victim is literally hurled into oncoming traffic in a crowded city street. According to one report, over thirteen hundred people were killed by this method in a single year in the city of Okayama.

They are into violence. When one

Yakuza boss picked a fight with a 27-year-old student in Kobe, a port south west of Tokyo, seven of his underlings joined in and kicked the innocent young man half to death, before carrying his body onto the street and finishing the job there.

They are even into karaoke: one of

their leading syndicate bosses is said to include in his repertoire an extremely good rendition of the ballad set to the theme of perhaps the most famous gangster movie of all time – *The Godfather*.

If there's money to be made in it, the Yakuza are into it!

The name 'Yakuza' means 8-9-3, Ya meaning eight, *Ka* nine and *Za* three, and comes from the Japanese equivalent of the gambling game Blackjack, *Oicho-Kabu*. In Blackjack, the aim is to get three cards that total twenty-one. In Oicho-Kabu the top hand totals nineteen. Ya, Ka and Za

Boeing 747 of Japan Airlines lifts off from Tokyo Airport. In 1999, Japanese police uncovered the Yakuza connections of one of the airline's biggest investors.

total twenty and the hand is, therefore, quite worthless.

The Yakuza, whose origins can be traced back to 1621, when men known as *kabuki-moni* (the crazy ones) by their detractors came to the attention of the authorities because of their defiance of the Samurai, the powerful, often murderous warlords who controlled Japan. The Samurai considered them as worthless, just like an Oicha-Kabu hand made up of Ya, the Ka and the Za. No one knows who applied the sobriquet to the wild, young men. But someone (probably a Samurai or other member of the shogunate) did, and the name stuck.

Despite their defiance and their willingness to wield their long swords to express their hatred of the Samurai and Shoguns, the *machi-yakko* acquired a Robin-Hood-like status among the ordinary Japanese, something that alarmed the shogunate so much that they began rounding the young rebels up and executing them. By 1686, according to Kanehiro Hoshino of Japan's Police Science Research Institute, the last of them had been put to the sword.

Tales of their exploits were handed down, becoming folk tales and the stuff of which several kabuki plays were made, and in the mid-eighteenth century the first of the 'modern' Yakuza appeared.

In the same way that thousands of miles away, in Sicily, the Mafia came to be organized, the Yakuza gangs were divided into families. In Japan, this mirrored the traditional *oyabun-kobun* or father-son relationship. (Anyone who detects a similarity

between not just the name but the relationship between a certain *Obi-wan Kenobi* and his protege Anakin Skywalker in the *Star Wars* movies, will not be surprised to learn that George Lucas, whose brainchild the series was, has a wide knowledge of all things Japanese.)

By using the tradition that in the Japanese family, the father was (and to some extents still is) the authority figure, the Yakuza achieved strength and cohesion. The master holds absolute power over the apprentice – no questions asked. As one adage has it, 'If he says black is white, then black is white!'

Japan was probably the last country in the world to get rid of feudalism. While Europe and North America were starting to enjoy the benefits of industrialization, Japan remained a closed door: visitors were not welcome. It was not until 1871 when the re-established emperor issued an imperial decree abolishing the local autonomy that had allowed the shogunate to dominate Japan for centuries and maintain their grip on society. The feudal system was swept away and foreigners were welcomed. The British built railways and helped the Japanese to reorganize their navy. The Americans supervised a new postal system. The French recast the legal system and helped train Japanese soldiers. The Germans assisted with the development of medicine and local government. And the Yakuza began to infiltrate the booming construction industry, the docks, the rickshaw business, recruiting members into their number. They also retained their traditional interests in running prostitution, gambling, extortion, drugs and street peddling.

The bosses of several factions of the Yakuza, the *bakuto*, organized legitimate businesses, fronts to cover their illegal activities. At the same time, the leaders of the *tekiya*, the factions that controlled countless thousands of peddlers' stalls in cities, towns and villages throughout the country, cultivated important ties to politicians and police chiefs – 'cultivated important ties' being a euphemism for bribery.

It was around this time, that an ex-Samurai, Toyama Mitsuru, joined an ultra right-wing and nationalist group, the *Kyoshish*a. He gradually began to attract his own following, which led him a few years later to found his own organizaion, the *Genoyosha* ('The Black Dragon – or Dark Ocean – Society'), a federation of existing nationalist groups, which went on to become the progenitor of modern secret societies.

Genoyosha members got jobs as bodyguards for local politicians and also in the trade union organizations, pursuing their right-wing agenda at home and abroad. They were responsible for attacks and the assassinations of countless politicians whom they regarded as dangerously left wing. In 1892, Mitsuru forged an alliance with the underworld to ensure that a right-wing government was returned, with the result that it was the bloodiest in Japan's history. He expanded the organization into China and Korea where, in 1895, it was responsible for the assassination of the Korean queen.

Genoyosha spawned hundreds of secret societies. True, some of them were sponsored by wealthy patrons who shared Toyama Mitsuru's political agenda and beliefs, but many of them were financed by the proceeds of prostitution, gambling, extortion, drugs and street peddling and the other standard criminal activities that had been, by tradition, the province of the Yakuza.

By now socialism was gaining a

Traditional Japanese Samurai garb.

toehold in the governments of other countries – anathema to the Genoyosha, and distinctly unattractive to the Yakuza gangs. They knew that it was much easier for them to influence right-wing politicians than idealistic left-wingers with their dreams of replacing corrupt political dealings with clean, open

*Strip bar, Tokyo, Japan. The Japanese sex industry
is a reliable money-spinner for the Yakuza.*

organization. Any political movement towards the left, in Japan, jeopardized their authority.

And so, as the rightist politicians became more involved in criminal activities to finance their operation, the Yakuza became more involved in right-wing politics and the distinction between the two blurred until they became almost indistinguishable.

The alliance between the two continued up to and after the Second World War. The Allied victory saw Japan occupied by American troops, who regarded the Yakuza as a threat and began to take an active interest in the organization, aiming to eradicate it. Though why, with the example of the US 'success' in dealing with the Mafia, they thought were street hustlers who took as their role models, not the noble Samurai of the past, but the sharp-suited, and sun-glassed heroes of the American gangster movies with which US distributors flooded Japanese cinemas – to the delight of the younger generation who were much more open to Westernization than their tradition-loving parents and grandparents whose deep shame of their country's defeat lingered for many years.

It wasn't just their appearance that changed. Swords were replaced with guns as the Yakuza adopted the methods of their American counterparts. The new style proved attractive to young Japanese. In 1958, Japanese police estimated that there were seventy thousand Yakuza in the country. By 1963, the number had more than doubled to one hundred and eighty-four thousand, making it by far the largest criminal organization in the world.

New Yakuza gangs were springing up all over Japan. Existing ones were swelling their numbers. The most feared of the ones that emerged after the War was the *Yamaguchi-Gumi*, based in Kobe. It was, according to the Japanese police, just another small-time waterfront mob, until Taoka Kazua appeared on the scene.

Taoka Kazua

Known as Japan's Al Capone or the 'Boss of Bosses', Kazua was born in 1913 on Shikoku, one of the large islands that make up much of the south of Japan. After his parents died, he was sent to work in one of the

they would have any more success with the Yakuza is something of a paradox.

The Americans rationed food. This only served to increase the power of the Yakuza gangs. For with rationing came an active black market, and who ran it?

It was at this time that a new breed of Yakuza appeared. The *gurentai*

Kobe shipyards when he was fourteen. There he became involved with a gang headed by a mobster called Yamaguchi Noburu. For nine years he served his apprenticeship with the gang, earning the nickname 'The Bear', thanks to his rough fighting skills, before becoming a fully-fledged, blood member in 1936 when he was sent to prison for slashing a member of a rival gang to death.

He was released in 1943, by which time the war had taken its toll on his and other Yakuza gangs in terms of size and influence. Three years later when Yamaguchi died, Taoka stepped into his shoes. Using a combination of his fearsome ferocity and brilliant organizational abilities he set about organizing the members that remained. He founded the Yamaguchi-gumi Construction Company in Kobe docks, seeing to it that it was awarded all major building contracts, which were many in post-war Japan. At the same time he took the lion's share in local extortion rackets and gambling. He then started expanding his empire, at first locally, taking over the rival Kobe gang, Honda-kai, and later beyond, absorbing Osaka's Meiyu-kai and Miyamoto-gumi.

That was just the beginning. By 1964 he was the boss of three hundred and forty-three different gangs. He is believed to have controlled eighty per cent of all the cargo loading in Kobe's docks. As well as all the rackets he controlled – extortion, gambling, prostitution and the other standard gangland fare – he introduced the mob into the

Let's go to work: top members of the Yamaguchi guni, Japan's largest gangster 'family' attend the funeral for mobster Masahisa Takenaka.

entertainment business, founding a talent agency that promoted performers from the Osaka area, as well as a pop group called the Home Run Hit Parade. He used that as a lever to get the Yakuza into Japan's lucrative film industry and into the professional sporting world as well.

For thirty-five years, he was the godfather of Japan's criminal syndicates, with at least thirteen thousand Yakuza members owing him their loyalty. But it was not just the criminal underworld that he dominated. Right-wing politicians, including one of the most powerful men in Japan, Kodama Yoshio, backed him. In return for this, Taoka's men were put at their disposal in their violent fight against communism.

Kodama worked for the Japanese government both before the war when he set up a massive spy network in China, during it when he bought and sold radium, copper and other metals and commodities vital to the Japanese war effort, often trading heroin for them. By 1945 his empire was worth $175 million, making him so powerful that he was made a rear-admiral!

After the war, and after serving two years in prison for war crimes, Kodama increased his power base and made himself useful to the Americans – often to their cost as in 1949 when the CIA paid him $150,000 to smuggle a shipload of tungsten out of China. The cargo was never delivered. Kodama told the CIA that the ship sank during the voyage across the Sea of Japan. That didn't stop him pocketing the money!

From the beginning of his career, Kodama had used his Yakuza connections, and it was inevitable that his path should cross with the increasingly powerful Taoka Kazuo. He introduced Taoka to Machii Hisayuki, the Korean-born boss of Tokyo's most important Yakuza gang, the Tosei-kai ('Voice of the East Gang'). This allowed Taoka to expand into Tokyo, something increased his operations considerably. By the time he died in 1981, his businesses had an annual turnover of £460 million.

Another Yakuza marriage that Kodama brokered was the one between Yokohama's Kakusei-kai gang and the Inagawa-kai. It took him nine years of careful planning and by the time it was complete, in 1972, Kodama, was one of the most powerful men in Japan. But he became mired in 1976 when it emerged that he had been given $2.1 million by the Lockheed Corporation to use his influence to get Japanese airlines to buy its TriStar L1011. The revelation prompted accusations of $6 million tax evasion, something that so upset one of his admirers, a young actor called Mitsuyasu Maeno, to crash his plane into Kodama's house in Setagaya, an affluent Tokyo suburb.

Maeno died in the crash: Kodama survived only to be indicted for bribery, perjury and breach of the exchange laws. He died of a stroke before he came to trial.

Inagawa Kakuji

Inagawa has been called the elder statesman of the Japanese

underworld and believes that the day will come when all the Yakuza gangs merged into what he calls 'one mob'. The process by which the bigger gangs take over the smaller ones, and the larger ones merge with each other, which has been going on for some time, will continue. And in the language of the business strategist he says, 'You can see the move towards a more corporate structure.'

During the Second World War, Inagawa was the brains behind a small street gang in Yokohama that did what it could to muscle in on the activities of the Chinese and Korean gangs that controlled much of the city's black marketeering. Not only did he come to the attention of Tsuruoka Masajiro, the city's godfather who took the young thug under his wing, he was also spotted by the occupying authorities. In 1950, the US Consul-General in Yokohama cabled Washington DC, warning his superiors of the dangers that he and his gang posed

By 1960, the gang now known as

Cartoon pornography in one of Tokyo's many sex shops.

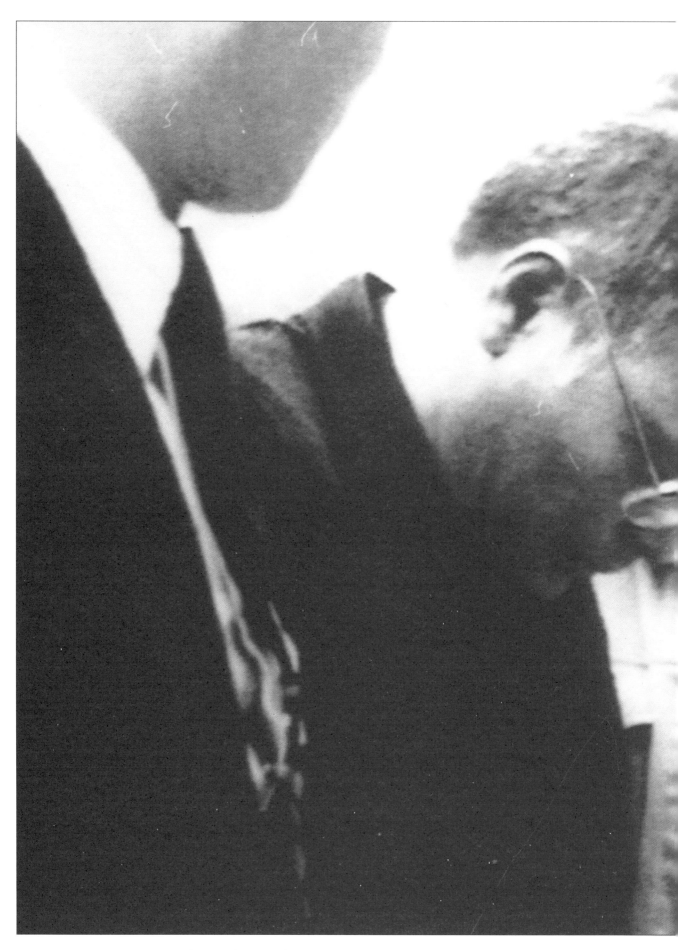

Prominent Yakuza member Seiki Nakagawa is arrested by detectives working out of the Osaka Police headquarters November 1986.

the Kakusei-kai had spread from Yokohama to Tokyo and beyond, into Hokkaido, Japan's main northern island. Gambling was by now its main business, with Inagawa almost single-handedly in control of the lucrative casino gambling rackets, which made him a fortune: his fee from one card game alone was estimated by the Tokyo police to have been $175,000.

After suffering years of police harassment, he changed the gang's name to Kinsei-kai, petitioning the Japanese government, which in its efforts to keep communism out often overlooked the Yakuza's activities, to give his gang political status.

Pushing for alliances with other Yakuza gangs, Inagawa said, 'If we unite and become a wall to stop communism we can be of service to the nation.' But he had to wait several years for his dream to come true, for he was arrested in the mid-1960s and held in Japan's Fukushima Prison until early 1969. By the time he was released his Kinsei-kai had been overtaken by the Yamaguchi-gumi gang as the most powerful of all the country's Yakuza. It was Kodama Yoshio who forged an alliance between the two giving the Yamaguchi-Inagawa brotherhood effective control of all but four of Japan's metropolitan areas.

By the late 1970s, the syndicate had branched out from gambling into drug dealing, all forms of vice and loan-sharking. A network of an estimated 879 legitimate businesses from building companies to restaurants front the gang's illegal activities and is thought to have added $200 million to its coffers.

Gamblers Anonymous: slot-machine punters feed their obsession – and the machines.

Inagawa runs his gang like a captain of industry runs his business. There are twelve 'directors' on the board, representing one hundred and nineteen gangs, overseen by Inagawa from his plush Tokyo hotel suite. He moves in the highest circles, mixing with the top men in commerce, business and entertainment. He has access to top Tokyo policemen, many of whom attend the golf tournaments on two Mondays every month, where they rub shoulders with sports and film stars – fitting company for the man on whom the 1984 movie *Shura no Mure*, the Japanese equivalent of *The Godfather*, was based. Not bad for someone who started off as a small-time gangster in the streets of Yokohama.

Kakuji believes that the Yakuza will eventually become like the Mafia in the United States. 'In the future,' he is on record as saying, 'there'll be one national mob.'

Yakuza structure

At the street level, there are two kinds of Yakuza – the freelance and the clan. Freelance Yakuza are petty criminals who operate at street level, usually on their own, but sometimes they get together to work small-time rackets. But life as a freelance Yakuza is dangerous. If they come up against a clan, at best their activities will be brought to the attention of the police and they will find themselves in prison, often for crimes they didn't commit. At worst they simply vanish without trace, their bodies perhaps washed up near the docks, or on a rubbish tip in a seedy part of town.

Clan-yakuza are like the Sicilian Mafia families, who are responsible for the rackets in the area they control. They are usually associated with a larger clan and as such are the small cogs in the wheels that are the major crime cartels in Japan. Small clans sometimes call upon the services of the freelance yakuza they detest so much, if there is work to be done with which they do not want to be associated.

Like the Mafia, the Yakuza is an all-male society with its own structured hierarchy. At the head of each clan is an *Oyabun*, or father, whose word is law to those beneath him. Reporting to him there are usually two Yakuza of equal rank to each other but with their own function. The *Saiko-komon* runs the organization's secretariat and has a 'bookkeeper', 'advocate' and 'secretary' working for him. At the same level as the *Saiko-komon* is the *Waka-gashira* controlling the activities of ordinary gang members.

Things are complicated by the fact that some of the men in a clan may be the Oyabun of a clan of his own. The activities of these brother clans are overseen in the clan to whom the junior Oyabun owes allegiance by the *Shati-gashira*. These minor Oyabun are referred to as *Kyodai* in the superior clan, and the Yakuza they control are called *Shatei*. The fact that these Shatei may also be Oyabun of their own clans makes the overall structure a hopeless maze for Japan's police to penetrate, a fact compounded by the vow of silence that is demanded from each clan member.

Many Yakuza decorate their bodies with elaborate tattoos. The initial one is usually a black ring around one or other arm, which is done to mark the first crime perpetrated by a Yakuza member. A new ring is added for each subsequent misdemeanour. Then as more and more crimes are committed, more and more designs are tattooed on to the Yakuza's body, until there is little room for any more. Some of the more elaborate designs can take up to 100 hours to complete.

It's not just the number of tattoos that can mark out a Yakuza man. Many of them have the top part of a finger missing. This is the result of self-mutilation, something a Yakuza will do if he fears he has offended a superior member of his clan. The finger tip is wrapped in tissue and sent to whoever has been offended with a plea for forgiveness.

The practice has its origins in the history of Japanese gambling. When someone could not pay his gambling debts, the debtor could demand the tip of a finger by way of recompense. This originated at a time when gambling was illegal in Japan and anyone seen with a fingertip missing was immediately suspected of having taken part in an illicit game.

Like their counterparts in the American Cosa Nostra and the Sicilian Mafia, the Japanese Yakuza has been the focus of police clamp-downs in recent years, but such is their control over crime in Japan, and such is their influence in the upper echelons of the police, big business and politics, and such is its appeal to the lowlife of the major Japanese cities, that it is more than likely that the Yakuza will continue to flourish for the foreseeable future – and beyond!

5 THE RUSSIAN MAFYA

THE Russian Mafia is usually called the 'Mafya' to distinguish it from the Sicilian Mafia and American Cosa Nostra. Its rise to the dominant position it holds in the criminal world of Russia and other parts of the world is thought by many to be a recent phenomenon.

Not quite true. Organized crime flourished in the Soviet Union where anything could be bought on the black market. The rewards were high – hard currency. The punishment was higher: years in a Soviet gulag or death – which was worse is a matter of opinion.

But it was only when communism collapsed in the late 1980s that the Mafya emerged from the shadowy world in which syndicated crime was organized in Russia. And in the wave of freedom that swept through the USSR and the satellite countries of Eastern Europe, the Russian gangs that make up the Mafya, and the criminals who ran them, found that they had almost as much power and economic clout as the states themselves.

The reason for this is that after years of operating under communism, the Mafya was more organized than the fledgling political groups who found themselves in power but ill-equipped to handle it. And now able to cross national borders without restraint, Mafya gangs were able to put their roots down and flourish in the new democracies of Eastern Europe. From there they began to operate throughout Europe and other countries of the world.

The official line on Russia's future was that after the fall of communism, the country was going to be one of the major and most enterprising economic powers of the world: a nation like its old enemy the United States; a nation with a booming economy fuelled by high wage earners.

But the transition from state-dominated monolith to free-enterprise Utopia was not to be – at least not yet. For the reality is that life for the average Russian has hardly changed. The Russian people may have had little faith in communism, but the system that replaced it has done little to improve their lot. Political power still lies in the hands of a small elite, and corruption

The spires of the Kremlin loom over Moscow's Red Square.

flourishes at every level of government, national and local.

Leadership is what is needed, but
years of communism have sucked the
people dry of the forward-looking
individuals who could help Russia
take the step forward that is required.
The Mafya has such people, and, with
the fall of the old system, they found
themselves with the golden opportunity of being able to offer those
who were attracted to it at least some
of the prosperity they were seeking.
At a price of course: like all gangs,
once in there is no way out.

Mark Galeotti, an acknowledged

Russian anti-racketeering police task force detains Mafya suspects, Moscow, 1996

expert in organized crime in Russia, has identified different types of Mafya groupings. Many of these gangs have 'formal' structures. At the top is the *pakhan*, the boss, and the man whose word is law. He runs four cells, each headed by a brigadier. One cell plans the gang's operations,

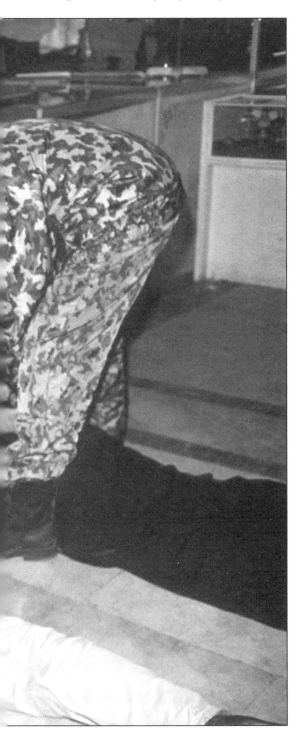

another looks after security and the other two perpetrate the actual crimes.

At the bottom of the ladder there are the old-fashioned mobsters running traditional mob rackets – prostitution, protection and robbery. Many of them are over-confident and sloppy and their crimes are easily detected, so they end up in prison. Either that, or they are assassinated by members of a rival gang, perhaps as a result of a deliberate attempt on their lives, or they are gunned down in one of the many battles fought on the streets of Russia's towns and cities between rival gangs. If they survive life at the lower level, many of these gangsters are often taken on as musclemen by larger and better-organized gangs.

Galeotti's second group is the specialist money launderer and what he calls 'gangs within gangs'. These may be corrupt police officers or members of the military who augment their meagre salaries by selling weapons, offering themselves as high-quality 'protectors' and even as hit men.

The next rung up is formed by the white-collar criminals, Mafya gangsters posing as businessmen, whose respectable fronts cover up the wide range of criminal activities that they control. At the start of the new millennium, the authorities reckon not just that over forty thousand legally formed companies were fronts for Mafya activities, but that half the Russian banks were run by Mafya groups.

And at the top are the big men who sit on the equivalent of the Mafya's

Ex-Russian premier Boris Yeltsin meets the people at a traditional Russian spring festival, 1996.

national council – the *vory y zakonye*. They are the major wheeler-dealers, the arbitrators, the men who rub shoulders with the great and the good of Russia's political and social scene.

When Communism retreated, it was the men on the vory y zakonye who saw the opportunity this presented and grasped it with both hands, to the extent that some experts believe, that if the Russian economy has started to improve over the last few years, it is thanks to the Mafya. For like their brothers in other countries where organized crime flourishes, they have put in place politicians who do as they are told. Mafya leaders have turned to legitimate businesses using the proceeds of Mafya criminal activities and from their well-protected multi-million Euro houses on the Cap d'Antibes and other elite locations Mafya leaders run networks of legal and illegal businesses that are impossible to disentangle.

In 1991, Mafya leaders met to discuss future strategy and over the following four years the number of organized crime groups rose from two thousand to five thousand and the crime rate in Russia by over half. Moscow was the battlefield for the struggle for dominance between the Chechen Mafya with around fifteen and a half thousand members and the same number of allies in other Mafya gangs, and the Georgian gangs who were under the control of Otari Kvantrishvili.

A gangland thug from an early age, he served only two years of a ten-year sentence for rape, being released on mental health grounds. Behind the respectable façade he adopted (he was coach to the Russian Olympic wrestling team and established a charity for the widows and fatherless children of dead policemen), he was rising rapidly up the Mafya hierarchy. He invested money in a casino (the first hard-currency one on Moscow) and in a chain of shops, in which he also sold stolen goods.

Such was his influence that in 1993 one of his companies was given a two-year tax exemption by none other than the Russian president,

Mafya members celebra

Boris Yeltsin. In August the same year, Kvantrishvili's brother tried to muscle in on the protection of a powerful businessman who was already being 'looked after' by a Chechen gang. There had been trouble between the two rival gang

tal, Ekaterinburg, 1997.

cultures in the previous few weeks. In July, seven armed men, armed with pistols and assault rifles, had burst into the Alfa Romeo dealership headquarters to settle a dispute over protection money. In the ensuing battle two guards and two gunmen were killed. The following day, the dispute escalated when three more men were shot dead during a gun-fight in a restaurant known to be a Mafya hangout.

In February 1994 five more Muscovite gangsters were shot in one or other of the increasingly common gun battles that were fought in Moscow's streets. And in St Petersburg, ten more were shot dead, their bodies dragged to nearby woodland, doused in petrol and put to the flame.

By this time, Kvantrishvili's brother had been accounted for by Chechen marksmen. And on 5 April 1994 Kvantrishvili was assassinated by the bullet, outside a Moscow bathhouse. Gangsters and polite Moscow society rubbed shoulders at his funeral.

To this day, no one knows who was responsible for the assassination. It could have been someone from the Dolgroprudny gang, from northwest Moscow, which specialized in protection. It might have been a mobster from southeast Moscow's Lyubertsky gang, which specialized in prostitution, extortion and contract murders and whose members were known to beat up punk rockers and hippies just for the hell of it. Or was it someone from the Solntsevo gang from south of the city, from where its leader and his men ran slot-machine and protection rackets? If it was the latter then it could be that Kvantrishvili's men had their revenge, for a few months after his death, their leader was killed when his Mercedes was booby-trapped to such devastating effect that he was identified only from dental records.

The police found and still find themselves unable to solve Kvantrishvili's and other Mafya members' murders for several reasons. Not only are they under-funded, many of the men high up in the police hierarchy are in the pay of Mafya gangs. There is a lack of dedicated, qualified people to take up the challenge that the Mafya presents.

But perhaps the most telling reason for the Mafya's success is the effect that communism had on Russia. Years of living under Soviet rule has bred in the majority of the Russian people a cynical opinion of authority. This saps any strength there may have been on the part of the ordinary man in the street to take on what they see as just another big organization like the one that controlled their lives for so long.

The Mafya flourishes all over Russia, with gang warfare rife. In St Petersburg, in the early years of the 1990s there were street gunfights between native city-born gangsters who ran extortion, protection and the other usual Mafya rackets and men who owed their loyalty to Nikolai Zaikov. Also known as Yakutionok, he was a mobster from the Urals who had his eye on controlling the fledgling but hugely profitable designer drug industry.

In the Siberian city of Sverdlovsk, formerly known as Ekaterinburg, where Nicholas II and the Russian imperial family were assassinated in 1918, the Uralmash gang ran things until 1992. Then gangs of Caucasians and Mafya mob known as the *Tsenteral'nayas* tried to muscle in for control of crimes involving the theft of oil and the precious metals that are mined in the area.

In the far east of the country, control of the widespread smuggling and counterfeiting scams was the area of contention between Yevgeni Petrovich Yasim and Chinese gangs.

In the south, in the Crimea, where many politicians and other Russians with the means to do so enjoy the summer sun, are two Mafya mobs, the Salem gang and the Bashmakis, founded by the now dead Bash-makov brothers. On a local level, the gangs force garages and restaurants to pay protection money, and extort money from the many illegal businesses that flourish in the area. They also have a hand in the off-shore oil and gas industries.

The Crimean Mafya, like their fellow mobsters in other parts of the country are expert at the practice known as *krysha*. In a country where to enforce a debt through the courts is a long and laborious process, and the incorruptibility of court officials cannot be taken for granted, many firms pay the Mafya up to thirty per cent of their profits to collect outstanding debts and to enforce contracts.

Even by Mafya standards, the Crimean gangs are ruthless: in one year alone, 1995, there were seventy-five unsolved contract killings. In the years that followed, the man charged

*Russian prostitutes, Paris. The Mafya is known to be heavily involved
in transporting women from Eastern Europe to the West to work in the sex industry.*

with fighting organized crime in the area, Colonel Nikolai Zverev, was bludgeoned to death with a piece of lead piping as he strolled home after parking his car close to his house. Three local politicians who spoke out against the Mafya were assassinated. Others who were targeted during the Crimean Mafya's reign of terror were luckier. One local political leader survived the stab wounds to his chest that he received when Mafya thugs attacked him. The mayor of Sebastopol also escaped an attempt on his life, counting himself lucky when he walked from the debris caused by a bomb explosion having lost a finger. And the leader of the local *duma* (or city council) was convinced that he was going to be assassinated when he was kidnapped. But he was released three days later when the ransom that the Mafya gang responsible demanded was paid.

The Mafya abroad

Being so successful at home, it's little surprise that the Mafya has put down roots in Europe and America. It has forged links with the Cosa Nostra and Sicilian Mafia and, what is even more alarming to the authorities, with terrorist groups around the world; for the Mafya claim to be able to get their hands on nuclear materials. And these claims are probably true.

By the turn of the millennium, Mafya experts reckon that Russian gangsters were operating not just in the old Russian satellite countries of

The Bank of New York, reported in 1997 to have been the channel for billions of tainted dollars from a Russian crime mob.

Eastern Europe, but all over Western Europe, too. In London and the other capital cities they were laundering money on a huge scale; it is said with the active participation of former KGB officers. Property was the main attraction in London. The Mafya would use dirty money to buy shares and property ('placing'). Within a short time, that was sold, the proceeds plus money made from legal activities ('layering') to buy more shares or a larger property. This, in turn was sold, the proceeds again mixed ('integrated') with more clean money, by which time the money was well and truly laundered and beyond the long arm of the law.

London was also a centre of Mafya drug-running and fraud. Paris was another centre for laundering and also for prostitution, girls from Eastern Europe being brought there on false promises of proper job opportunities and being forced onto the streets when they arrived in the city. (Interestingly, the Mafya has said that in London, competition from local girls and young women from northern towns who come to the capital for a night or two each week to ply their trade was too strong to make it worth their while getting involved in prostitution there.) France is also a centre for Mafya drug-dealing. It is more or less certain that having forged links with Colombian drugs barons to smuggle drugs into Europe (the Mafya paid for the drugs with former Russian military equipment), Russian gangs took advantage of the strain that the invasion of hundreds of thousands of soccer fans from all over the world for the 1998 World Cup put on French immigration authorities to bring massive amounts of narcotics into the country.

Elsewhere in Europe, Italy is used for drug-running and the new and increasingly popular crime of 'people smuggling' – bringing illegal immigrants into the country. In Belgium, car theft is the name of the Mafya's game, which is also a major activity in Germany along with drugs and money laundering.

Switzerland is used solely for money laundering and even then it is believed only in very limited quantities. The reason for this is that in the 1970s and '80s, the Swiss authorities were accused of a lack of vigilance about letting criminals, especially Turkish heroin dealers, deposit large amounts of money in bank accounts there. They not only used Swiss banks as a safe refuge for their ill-gained money; some of the gangs involved ran their businesses from offices in Swiss cities.

When the Swiss realized that there was a threat that some Russian Mafya men might try to base their activities in Switzerland, they decided to clamp down. One of the first to suffer, in 1996, was then 38-year-old Sergei Mikhailov, known as 'Mikhas' who was suspected as being the 'godfather' of the Solnstevskaya, one of the biggest criminal organizations in Russia.

Mikhailov settled in Switzerland in 1995 and within a few months had established a string of companies, each one with men and women of irreproachable character and reputation on the board and each one soon with more than healthy balances in the bank accounts they held.

Suspicious that large-scale money laundering was afoot, the Swiss arrested Mikhailov. His lawyers protested that he was a perfectly honest and respected businessman, who had also donated large amounts of money to various Swiss charities. Not so, claimed the Swiss, who said they had evidence that Mikhailov was involved in criminal associations in Russia. When his lawyers showed there was no such crime in Russia, where it is almost impossible to institute criminal proceedings against someone who has not been caught red-handed, the Swiss had no alternative other than to release the Russian. But the experience seems to have acted as a lesson to the Russian Mafya to limit their operations in the country.

But if the Swiss are extra-vigilant about Mafya money-laundering activities, the same it cannot be said about the Caribbean islands of Antigua, St Maarten and Aruba. Banking regulations there not being especially strict (although they have been tightened in recent years as part of the fight against the international drugs trade) make the islands a popular destination for Mafya money.

The Mafya is also active in Israel where, until the arrival of Russian gangsters, organized crime had been much the same as it was in other countries: local gangs running protection rackets, frauds and scams, with the outbreaks of gangland killings when there was a breakdown in local discipline, a new mob tried to muscle in on an old one's territory or as punishment for betrayal.

Things started to change with the establishment of drug-running networks in the early 1970s to supply the demand for heroin that came in from Turkey and Europe. This saw an upsurge in crimes like burglary as addicts turned to theft to pay for their habit. At the same time there was an increase in organized and systematic bank robberies, diamond heists and warehouse thefts, the proceeds from all of which was invested in the drug trade and in legal businesses to be used for money laundering.

But from the late 1970s with the relaxation on emigration controls on Jews living in Russia there was an increase in the numbers of Russian Jews emigrating, and later, between 1988 and 1995 more than six hundred and fifty thousand Jews left Russia for Israel and with them went the Mafya.

At the lowest levels of Israeli crime, Mafya gangs are involved in localized lucrative forgery scams, illegal gambling, money-lending and extortion and drug-dealing.

At a higher level are gangs involved in what Israeli police call 'local international crime': gangs whose activities are overseen by Mafya leaders in Moscow, St Petersburg and other Russian centres and much of whose revenues are diverted back to Russia. As well as overseeing prostitution, locally recruited 'soldiers' use whatever means necessary to muscle in on local crime and 'persuade' the owners of illegal casinos and other nefarious gambling activities to enter into partnerships with the Mafya.

The Russian-based gangs are also involved in a heartless scam that defrauds innocent immigrants of the grants they receive to help them be absorbed into Israeli society. These 'absorption packages' can be worth up to £40,000, making it a very profitable operation.

At the top level of Mafya activity in Israel, vast amount of money, much of it illegally obtained, had been invested in Israeli banks (£2.5 billion) and in property (£400 million). These are estimated figures for 1997. By now, it is probably much, much more.

The Mafya in the United States

A study of Russian Organized Crime (ROC) in the United States, where there are estimated to be at least fifteen Mafya gangs with 8,000 members, revealed a great deal about the structure – or lack of it – of the Mafya. There, and most probably in the other countries where the organization operates, the gangs are neither centralized nor dominated by a small number of individuals. The men who do wield power, do so because of their personal characteristics: when they 'retire' (or are eliminated) another such person steps into his shoes. And so the network lacks continuous structure.

But it is clear that the gangs are not simply small groups of criminals acting independently of one another, running extortion rackets and other traditional Mafya rackets at a local level. Instead there is what the FBI calls 'a broad connectivity' among the actors. They are not directly connected to a large number of others, but they are individually connected to some of them. This makes for flexibility in organizing criminal activities, making the gangs and gangsters able to respond quickly to opportunities for illegal operations as they develop. A member of one network who, for instance, needs money-laundering skills but lacks them can easily acquire them from another.

This makes for a very functional, if informal, structure – and a violent one. For with no formal hierarchy, there is no effective control of violence being used to settle the disputes that invariably develop. And the lack of formal sub-groupings weakens loyalty to past partners. One FBI report noted the high number of murders that occurred where the victim and assassin had once worked together in the same gang.

A major difficulty in bringing Mafya criminals to justice is that likely witnesses, including the victims, refuse to co-operate in investigations. In 1995, the report of the 'Tri-State Joint Soviet Emigré Organization Crime Project' that studied violent crime in New York, New Jersey and Pennsylvania concluded that 'of some seventy murders or attempted murders over a fifteen-year period, the victim, the perpetrator or both were involved in ongoing ROC activity. There was evidence in many of the cases to indicate that the victim was attacked as a result of a dispute between individual criminals or gangs, or in retaliation for a prior violent act.' The majority of the crimes they investigated involve the use of guns, including automatic, semi-automatic and silencer-equipped handguns. But 'witnesses to the crimes could not be found or, if they could, neither they nor the victims would co-operate.'

Violence is a hallmark of the Mafya: it is used to gain control of criminal activities in an area and to maintain it – hardly surprising when one considers that extortion and protection rackets are the staples of the Mafya's activities. They are also involved in prostitution, drug running, contract murder, art theft, and arson against businesses whose owners refuse to pay protection money. They are also adept at adapting to circumstances and diversifying into new criminal activities. Mafya gangs are extensively involved in a variety of scams and frauds – health care swindles, antiques thefts, tax-evasion schemes, identity theft – challenging the West African gangs who are the international leaders in this particular crime for the Number One spot.

The Mafya Down Under

It's much the same story on Australia, where Russian and Eastern European gangs, particularly from Romania, have emerged as a frightening new force in the underworld. They have become the major players in Melbourne's heroin trade and rule over their fellow countrymen with an iron fist. Many of the Russian gangs have links with the New York Mafya.

In 2002, Victoria's prime minister Andre Haermeyer said that the police had seen the Irish and Italians dominate the crime scene in the state, particularly in Melbourne, the state capital. The Triads had dominated for a time, but now, with the Iron Curtain coming down, 'there has now been rise of an underworld organization, what's referred to as the Russian Mafya. We have got to deal with this sort of organized crime and...we need to acknowledge that there are networks.' He went on to describe how well organized and ruthless they were. 'They're a group of people that associate with each other. People give orders and they go ahead and do whatever they're told to do.'

The Mafya in Australia are heavily involved in extortion, drug trafficking, large commercial business burglaries and passport fraud, 'anything to do with making money by doing as little as possible'.

'They are very violent because they have come from a very violent and a very troubled past,' a senior policeman in Melbourne said. 'They're a problem and they're only going to get worse. When the Russian criminals say, "I'm going to kill you," they mean it.'

As in the United States, indeed everywhere the Mafya is powerful, victims are loath to come forward and give evidence. 'In Russian culture, it's just part of everyday life that you have to pay protection or extortion money. And they've brought that culture with them.'

Fortunately for law-abiding Australians (and Australia's native criminals) the Mafya tend to target their own. In one particularly shocking crime, a balaclava-clad man

A rare photograph of the elusive Semion Mogilevich (date uncertain).

The headquarters of Magnex-2000, a Hungarian company that makes magnets, owned by the enigmatic leader of the Red Mafia, 52-year-old Ukrainian Jew Semion Mogilevich.

burst into a Melbourne motel room where Russian-Bulgarian gangster Nilolai Radev was holed up with three Australian associates and gunned the Eastern European thug down. As the other three cowered in terror, waiting for the gunman to turn his semi-automatic weapon on them, he turned, headed for the door and said in a thick Russian accent, 'Relax. We don't kill your kind! Just our own.'

Going legal

Russian criminals moved out of Russia and into international organized crime at a time when more and more gang leaders had realized the advantages to be had from investing in legitimate businesses such as textiles and the movie industry,

Clever, creative accountancy makes it almost impossible to distinguish between the income generated by the legitimate business of the company and the proceeds of illegal activities being laundered. That said, there have been several spectacular successes from the authorities' point of view. In 2001, for example, four individuals and two companies were investigated and prosecuted in connection with the laundering of between two and seven billion dollars through the Bank of New York. How much of this was income from Mafya criminal activity in other parts of the world and how much was Mafya money being moved out of Russia to evade law enforcement and tax officials and to be invested in legal businesses is not known. But it made a huge dent in Mafya finances.

It's the blend of legal and illegal activities that make the Mafya such a difficult problem for the authorities in all countries where it operates. Officialdom may know very well that the chairman of this multi-billion rouble company, that multi-million pound concern or that multi-million dollar industry is a Mafya gangster. But without hard evidence – evidence that is extremely hard to get – how can the authorities get behind the respectable facades of these Russian captains of industry and expose them for the criminals they are? For they not only have fear on their side, they have the men whose job it is to track them down in their pockets.

Who's who in the Mafya

So who are the men who have been accused of running organized crime in Russian – the big fish in the Mafya pond?

Let's start with Semion Mogilevich, a man who many reckon is the most powerful gangster in the world – not just today, but yesterday and perhaps tomorrow, too. He controls a network of legal and illegal businesses that stretch around the world.

He was born in 1948 in the Ukraine and is said to be inordinately proud of his Russian-Jewish heritage. Mogilevich first surfaced in the criminal world in the early 1970s when he was part of a gang that operated in the Moscow suburbs. Despite having a degree in economics, he shunned life as a civil servant, teacher or one of the other careers open to him, and turned to crime.

He made a living counterfeiting documents and as a petty thief. But he saw an opportunity when the old hard-line communist government began to soften just a little, enough to lift the emigration controls on the many Jews who wanted to leave the country and settle either in Israel or in the United States where many of them had relations. Mogilevich offered to buy their assets for hard currency, a pittance but enough to start a new life outside Russia. He made a vast profit from their sale.

He used much of the money he made by setting up a petrol exporting company with fellow Russian mobster Vyacheslav Ivankov, which was registered in the Channel Islands. Business prospered and by the start of the 1990s with communism now in retreat he had made a fortune. He moved to Israel, and from there established and controlled businesses in Prague as well as forging links with major 'businessmen' in California and New York. He later moved to Budapest, a shrewd move: he was by now an Israeli citizen of little interest to the Hungarian authorities who were more concerned with moving their country forward after years of stagnation under communist rule.

Still with many contacts in Russia, Mogilevich was one of the men who claimed to be able to supply nuclear materials not just to terrorist groups, but to developing-world governments which wanted them for peaceful purposes but lacked the resources to develop such materials themselves. At the same time he widened the scale of the rackets he controlled in Russia and in other Eastern European countries where he operated. It was not just the usual prostitution and drug running, but also jewellery heists and art thefts, which specialities that added to his already vast fortune.

Mogilevich formed an alliance with one of the many gangs in Moscow and established a network of art thieves that targeted museums and galleries at first in Moscow and St Petersburg, and then in other major Russian cities where there was art on display and security was lax. Alliances were then formed with other Mafya gangs throughout Eastern Europe where churches and synagogues were often richly decorated with jewelled icons and paintings of which there was little formal documentation. The local priest or rabbi may know the triptych on the wall was by this or that artist, or that there were valuable stones adorning a particular carved figure, but such is the richness and abundance of religious icons that it is an impossible task to catalogue them. But Mogilevich's men had their ears close to the ground and soon his warehouses in Budapest where he had established a legitimate jewellery and art restoration business were bulging with stolen artefacts.

Mogilevich kept the cream of it all to add to his own, priceless collection. Art was offered for sale on the black market if it was traceable, or if it was more anonymous given false provenance and sold to museums and collections all over the world. Jewellery was stripped down, the stones reset and the original settings being refurbished and sold at auctions and to dealers in countries from Argentina to Zaire.

But Mogilevich's greatest feat was to corner, quite legally, one hundred per cent of the Hungarian armaments trade. He did this by buying out a number of companies that made anti-aircraft artillery, and selling systems to the Hungarian army.

He has, it is believed, also used his contacts among high-ranking officers in the former USSR army to get his

Scud missile transporter. Rumours that the Mafya are offering the missiles for sale have become rife.

hands on nuclear materials: for with the break-up of the Soviet Union, such materials became easily available or at least not impossible to come by for someone of Mogilevich's wealth and stature. This has so worried NATO and the US that the FBI is negotiating with Hungarian authorities to open an office in Budapest: which would be the first

FBI field office outside the US.

Semion Mogilevich is also said to be actively involved in the international drugs trade, bringing illegal narcotics out of Asia and onto the markets of the world where its street value is hundreds of times greater than what the men who grown it receive. Already a multi-millionaire, probably a billionaire, by the early 1990s and before he is thought to have laid down a cent on drugs, Mogilevich bought a bankrupt airline to use as a means of getting the drugs out in large quantities.

Today it is impossible to hazard a guess at how much of the coke snorted at smart parties in affluent apartments in Adelaide, how much of the heroin injected into veins by addicts in the nooks and crannies of New York, how much of the crack cocaine inhaled in the gutters of Gateshead, started its journey out of the Golden Triangle in the holds of one of Mogilevich's freight planes or, swathed in a contraceptive and then swallowed by a 'mule' who took his or her place in the line at a third world airport to check in for a flight in an airliner owned by one of his companies.

It is rumoured that he has politicians from New York to New Delhi on his payroll, men well able to tip him off that an investigation is about to be launched into one or other of his activities, or that if he wants to move into a new area or activity than A, B or C would be a useful person (and one with a price) to get on board.

He has forged strong links with major Cosa Nostra families in New

York and Los Angeles, with the Camorra of Naples and other major gangs around the world.

Although he is probably based in Israel, the US is said to be the centre of his money-laundering operations. He has set up several successful multi-million dollar companies there on the east and west coasts, and no one knows how many shell companies he has in the area in between. Several of them have been investigated by the FBI and indictments have been issued, but Mogilevich is clever enough and has the contacts to ensure that his name has not appeared on any of them. It has been said that he has ensured this by offering to give Interpol and Europol incriminating evidence on other Mafya gangs. Such claims should be taken with a pinch of salt.

To paraphrase Shakespeare, he doth bestride the criminal world like a Colossus while other petty men walk under his legs and peep about to find themselves in dishonourable graves.

One of these 'petty men' but one still very much alive and kicking may be Grigory Lushansky. Is he the victimized businessman he claims to be, or is company he heads, Nordex, a front for Russian Mafya activities?

The Austrian-based company was capitalized at over two billion dollars in 1994, the year that Lushansky was photographed in Washington alongside President Clinton at a Democratic fund-raising dinner. The integrity and suitability of several people with whom the Democratic candidate had been mixing had been criticized by the Republicans. When Lushansky was seen at the event, one of them said, 'Here is another example of someone with an unsavoury background becoming involved in Democratic politics.'

His presence prompted former CIA director R. James Woolsey to recall that his then current successor in the post had told a congressional hearing to identify Nordex as 'an organization associated with Russian criminal activity'.

In the furore that followed, Newt Gringrich, the leader of the Republicans in Congress, said that the US government had determined that Lushansky was an international arms dealer who had shipped Scud missiles from North Korea to Iraq.

The day after Gringrich made his remarks, the *Washington Times* recalled a *Time Magazine* article of some months before. In it, Lushansky's Nordex company had been described as having been established to earn hard currency for the KGB and that since the fall of communism had been involved in nuclear smuggling, drug trafficking and money-laundering.

Lushansky denied any Mafya involvement. 'None of the US statements about links of this group of companies and with the criminal world is corroborated by facts and the results of numerous investigations which were carried out both by Russian and foreign secret services, including Interpol.'

Whether or not the accusations were true, the mud that flew was enough to make the Democrats withdraw an invitation to a subsequent event. Amy Tope, a Democrat spokesperson, said the Democrats had discovered some 'problems in his background and we let him know he was no longer invited'.

If the accusations are false, then Lushansky could have taken recourse to the courts to clear the stain on his company's name. If they are true and a Russian gangster was invited to stand alongside the President of the United States, it is frightening evidence of just how powerful the Mafya has become.

Evidence of this can be seen from at a party thrown to celebrate the opening of the first Estee Lauder boutique in Russia. The lavish party to mark the event was attended by Estee Lauder, the heir to the cosmetic company fortune, the president, Boris Yeltsin, the US ambassador, Thomas Pickering, and a glittering array of Moscow political and society figures.

The event was hosted by businessman Boris Bersozovsky, a dollar billionaire, who he claims was one of the six men who controlled the Russian economy when Boris Yeltsin was in power. He made his initial fortune from a car dealership he

founded as a jointventure with one of Russia's leading car manufacturers.

Within a few years his empire had extended to include oil, real estate, television stations and other media companies, and he was one of Boris Yeltsin's closest friends. When *Forbes* magazine accused him of having Mafya connections he sued and the case was settled out of court in his favour, the magazine withdrawing the claim.

When Yeltsin fell from power and was replaced by Vladimir Putin, Bersozovsky left Russia and sought political asylum in the United Kingdom, which was granted. But back in Russia he stands accused of being involved in a massive fraud, and should he ever visit Moscow, he would be arrested and put on trial.

There is no hard evidence that Bersozovsky had any Mafya connections, but there are many who believe it is unlikely that he rose to the position he did without having had some dealings with it. And that is symptomatic of the power of Mafya gangs not just in Russia, but all over the world.

6 GANGLAND UK

Organized crime is a comparatively recent phenomenon in the United Kingdom. There have always been gangs, of course, but when the Mafia was putting down its roots in Sicily, in Britain many of the sort of men to whom gang culture would have been attractive were otherwise engaged, serving in the army in the outposts of empire all over the world.

And when Sicilians and southern Italians emigrated from their homeland, it was to the United States that most of them went. That is why the Mafia is firmly established there, but has been kept at bay in the United Kingdom, mainly by the strict application of immigration laws that have seen several Mafia men either refused permission to enter the country, or deported if they managed to get in.

Other profitable activities that are or were illegal in some countries and therefore attract criminal gangs have been legalized in Britain, so there was little to gain to be made from them. When the streets of Chicago and New York were ringing to the rattle of machine-gun fire and gangsters were running illegal speakeasies, the British were enjoying their drink quite legally. Off-track gambling has been legal in Britain for decades, and today, the police more and more turn a blind eye to soft drugs.

That's not to say there were no gangs. In Glasgow, for example in the immediate post-war years, they prowled the streets in some parts of the city, armed with razors, which they were not afraid to use. Membership was often based on religion, for Glasgow is a city with a large Catholic population and a fervent Protestant one. The divide is most obvious in the city's two major football teams. Celtic was (and largely still is) supported by Catholics, while Glasgow Rangers has a huge following among the Protestant population.

If the gangs were involved in crime, it was at a petty level. Bit of housebreaking, maybe; small-time extortion and protection rackets; odd bit of pimping! Most of the trouble they caused was internecine and

South London gang boss Charles Richardson at the funeral of gangland 'enforcer' Lenny Maclean, August 1998.

usually over the territory they controlled. There was a similar situation in other cities, although the gangs that did rule the streets there were largely non-sectarian.

Things have changed.

British police estimate that there are around nine hundred criminal gangs in the UK. Many of them are involved in bringing illegal drugs into the country and distributing them in cities, towns and villages up and down the land. Lots of users can

afford to pay the prices charged for the designer drugs they use. Others cannot, and turn to petty crime to pay for the drugs they have to have.

Police estimate that drug trafficking in the UK generates around £8.5 billion a year. White and Colombian gangs are involved in narcotics, the latter mainly involved in cocaine. The trade in heroin is largely controlled by Turkish-Kurds. West Indian Yardies account for a large amount of the soft drugs brought into the country (and hard drugs, too) and are widely involved in their distribution.

Much of the vice in London and some illegal immigration are under the control of Albanian gangs. 'People smuggling' is the province of Chinese gangs, often with tragic consequences, evidenced by the twenty or so Chinese who suffocated to death in the back of the lorry that was bringing them illegally into the country. Nigerian gangs are heavily involved in fraud, particularly identity theft, and also in the illegal trade in 'bush meat'.

The fact that these are all comparatively recent developments and the fact that the gangs that did exist in post-war Britain were often little more than thorns in the flesh of the authorities is not to say that there were no big-time gangsters in the UK. There were, particularly in London.

'The Firm'

Say 'gangs' and 'London' to most people and two words will come to mind: Reggie and Ronnie, the Kray twins who, during the 1960s together with their brother Charlie, started what they called 'the Firm', one of the more notorious gangs in British history.

In October 1933, Violet Kray gave birth to two boys, Ronnie and Reggie, brothers for her first son, Charlie. The twins were identical but for one thing: the only way to tell them apart was the mole that Ronnie had just below his collarbone.

The East End of London at the time was dirty, rough, tough and dangerous – not the ideal place to grow up in, but the twins had their older brother and their mother to look out for them. The area became even more dangerous during World War II, when night after night, London was attacked by German aircraft, the East End bearing the brunt of the bombs. Ronnie and Reggie were evacuated to the country but only for a short time: the East End was like a magnet to them and it soon drew them back.

Their school in Daniel Street was often closed during the War, but even when it was open, the Krays only went when they wanted to – which was not all that often, and even when they did, they were more interested in picking playground fights than picking up their books. Fighting alongside each other they were an unbeatable combination.

It wasn't long before they graduated from the playground to the streets of the East End. They hung around corners, attacking pedestrians at random, sometimes to rob them, sometimes just for the hell of if. The police knew what they were up to, but arresting them was a problem: usually only one of the teenager twins did the actual assault. Establishing which one was impossible, the two were so alike!

When they were eventually arrested and put on probation, an experienced social worker succeeded in channelling the boys' energies into boxing, at the Mansford Amateur Boxing Club. They proved to be outstanding in the ring, their day jobs, lugging loads of fish around at the Billingsgate Fish Market, giving them the muscles they needed. They

Children play in a back street, East End of London.

were good enough to turn professional, but not sufficiently talented to make much of a career of it.

In 1950 the twins were called up for National Service. No sooner had they reported for duty at the Royal Fusiliers' recruiting centre at the Tower of London than they punched the sergeant in charge and hotfooted it back to the East End. Caught and returned in handcuffs to their barracks, as soon as they were there, they overpowered the guard and once again they scurried back to the East End.

They were picked up by the military police 24 hours later and returned to barracks. But there was no way that they were ever going to accept army discipline. Their behaviour was such that they were eventually court-martialled and sentenced to nine months in a military prison in Somerset, where they continued to flout authority, on one occasion ripping the red sash off one officer and emptying their slops bucket over him. When they had served their sentence, they were given a dishonourable discharge. Who was more relieved, the army to be rid of the twins, or the twins to be rid of the army, is hard to say.

Back in the East End, the twins went to work for would-be underworld boss, Jack 'Spot', so called because he was always on the spot when a crime was committed in the East End. Spot made his money from the rents he collected from bookmakers in the area – and from charging them protection money. He needed muscle to make his clients pay up. The twins had muscle and the happy knack of making Spot's tenants part with their money.

The Kray twins left Spot's employ after a short time when it became plain to them that he was losing the fight for control of the East End underworld to Billy Hill, boss of a rival gang. They set themselves up as freelance thugs and opened a snooker hall as their headquarters. The hall had been open for only a few days when a group of Maltese mobsters drove up and told them that if they didn't pay a fixed amount every week, 'something bad' would happen to the hall. Ronnie's answer was to rush the car and ram a bayonet through the roof. The Maltese mob drove off and never troubled the boys again.

In 1956 Ronnie was sentenced to three years for a vicious attack on an East End costermonger. Once inside, his behaviour was such that it became clear to the authorities that he was severely psychotic. Just after Christmas his mother, Violet, received a telegram from the governor of Winchester Prison where Ronnie was doing his time, stating bluntly, 'Your son Ronald Kray is certified insane.' She was later informed that her son had been sent to Long Grove Mental Hospital for an indefinite period.

Two years later, on one of his regular visits to see his brother, Reggie gave Ronnie the fawn overcoat he, Reggie, had been wearing when he arrived at the prison and told Ronnie to put it on. When it was time to go, it was Ronnie who was driven away from the prison and Reggie who was left inside. With

*Gangland glamour:
Ronnie and Reggie Kray
pose for the cameras
with Judy Garland
and friend.*

Ronnie was safely away, Reggie demanded to be let out, proving that he was not his twin, as he didn't have a mole beneath his collarbone.

Reggie made an appointment for his brother to see a top London psychiatrist under an assumed name. The doctor, not knowing whom it was he was examining, declared Ronnie sane.

But Ronnie's condition worsened and after he attempted to take his own life, his mother and two brothers did something quite unthinkable. They turned him in! When the police arrived to take him back to Long Grove, Ronnie went quietly without looking once at his family. Shortly afterwards he was declared fit to be released from hospital, and he served the rest of his sentence first in Winchester and later in London's Wandsworth Gaol.

While Ronnie was in prison, Reggie and Charles went into legitimate business, opening a drinking club, the Double R in an empty shop they rented in Bow Road. But it wasn't long before they regressed to their old ways, and when Ronnie was released they came up with the idea of 'the Firm' – an organization devoted to extortion, protection, forgery, drug running and gambling. The Firm started when the brothers opened an illegal gambling house in the top floor of the Double R. They then established the club as *the* place to drink in by making sure that the competition closed down. The mere threat of a visit from Ronnie the psychopath was often enough to see to that. (Later, the Double R was itself closed down after a police raid.)

Charlie and Reggie were also working as minders for fellow East Ender Billy Hill who had moved 'up West' where he was making his money (and lots of it) by arranging illegal gambling parties in Belgravia and Mayfair

Not long after Ronnie was released from prison, it became clear that the government was planning to legalize gambling in an effort to cleanse it of the criminal element with which it was tainted. Reggie reckoned that it would be the opportunity of a lifetime – a licence to print money. The new casinos would have to be run by someone, and who better than he and Charlie with the experience they had gained operating their own casino and working for Billy Hill? All they had to do was keep clean…

The fly in the ointment was Ronnie. He may have served his time, and been declared sane by the prison authorities, but it was quite clear that he was as dangerously mad as ever. He was so convinced of his invincibility that he had demanded protection money from slum landlord Peter Rachman, a particularly nasty and dangerous man. Rachman refused to pay, but knew he had to do something to get Ronnie Kray off his back. He arranged for Ronnie and his brothers to become involved in running Esmerelda's Barn, a newly licensed casino close to London's Hyde Park.

The money this made the Krays was a bonus to the £4,500 they were making each week by charging other West End casinos for their 'security services'

By the middle of the 1960s the Krays were swinging with the best of them (Ronnie particularly enjoying the new-found tolerance for homosexuals, and began to emerge from the closet.) They owned casinos and clubs; their rackets were bringing in thousands of pounds every month. They mingled with stars and politicians: the photograph of Ronnie with prominent Tory peer, Lord Boothby was one of the Krays' most prized possessions. And as if the money that was rolling in from gambling and protection was not enough, the Firm was also the London end of a Mafia stolen-bond laundering scam, earning a percentage of every deal.

Then things started to sour. Reggie's marriage fell apart, his young wife, Frances, claiming that her husband had abused her psychologically and physically. The divorce was long, bitter and public, and the publicity only became worse for Reggie when Frances committed suicide.

Among those following the newspaper stories about Reggie's divorce and Frances's death was Detective Inspector 'Nipper' Read, who had been taking an interest in the Firm's activities for some time.

Meanwhile, back in the East End, a rival gang run by John Richardson was attempting to muscle in on the Firm's territory. Richardson hoped to take control of the area by killing off certain of the Kray brothers' enforcers. But the plan backfired and after several shootouts in the area, Richardson was arrested and sent for trial. It was a public sensation. East Enders were all too aware of the activities of the gangs that operated in their area. To the rest of the country it was a bolt from the blue. Day after day as the trial proceeded, they read about gangland tortures, killings, blackmail, protection and extortion rackets.

Richardson and many of his men were given long sentences. The Krays, implicated but not directly involved, were now in 'Nipper' Read's sights.

One of Richardson's men who had escaped trial was George Cornell. The Krays suspected that he was bent on continuing Richardson's ambitions. On 9 March 1966, Ronnie and at least one of his henchmen sauntered into the Blind Beggar, a pub popular with East End gangsters. Three shots were fired. Two thudded into the ceiling. The third, from Ronnie's gun, took George Cornell in the head.

The police arrived on the scene within minutes, but knowing the way the East End worked, weren't too surprised to learn that nobody in the bar had seen had seen a thing!

Cornell was not the only victim of Ronnie Kray's madness. Nine months after he had shot the Richardson enforcer, Ronnie arranged for an old friend, Frank 'Mad Axe Man' Mitchell, to be sprung from his working party at HM Prison Dartmoor, where he was not long into a 32-year stretch for robbery with violence. It wasn't long, however, before Mitchell's constant whining began to grate on the twins' nerves. On Christmas Eve, Mitchell was told he was being taken from the Barking flat where he was staying to a safe house in the country for the holiday. No one knows if he woke up next day to see if Santa Claus had come: after being spotted in the back of a van speeding away from Barking he was never seen again.

The next of the Krays' known victims was one of their own strong-arm men, Jack 'The Hat' McVitie. He may have got off with bungling a contract killing – mistakes happen. But he should have known better that to start bad-mouthing the boys behind their backs and calling Ronnie 'a fat poof'. The twins invited McVitie to a party in a basement flat near Hackney. McVitie arrived to find the twins waiting. Reggie pulled a gun on him, but it jammed. McVitie made a run for it, but Reggie got to him and ended ' Jack the Hat's' life, stabbing him over and over again.

The East End knew what had happened. 'Nipper' Read knew what had happened. He established a team of fourteen detectives and set up a huge undercover operation aimed at nailing the Krays. He knew how the East End worked. He was only too well aware that nobody 'grassed' to the police, especially on thugs as powerful as the Krays, who appeared to have the entire area in a stranglehold. But Read had to get people to talk: how else could he get the evidence he would need to secure a conviction?

He knew there were many in the criminal underworld who had grudges against the twins – men who had suffered financially and physically at their hands. He and his team travelled as far afield as Canada to talk to them, but the evidence he

Sorted for E's and whizz: dancing the night away at a rave party.

needed was more than elusive. As one of the men involved in the Mafia scam said when Read interviewed him, without hard evidence, in court it would be one man's word against another's.

Read persuaded Scotland Yard to back the gamble he eventually decided to take: arrest the Krays before the case against them was in place, hoping that while they were on remand, witnesses would come forward. On 9 May, 1968, in a massive police operation, sixty officers swooped on 24 London addresses including Ronnie's and Reggie's flats, in the same apartment building. The twins put up no resistance. It would have been hard for them to do so: Reggie was in bed with a girl from Walthamstow and Ronnie with a rent boy from Bethnal Green.

The gamble paid off! Once the last of the Firm had been rounded up a few days later, tongues started to wag as London's underworld got its collective memory back.

At their trial, the twins, now 34, heard witness after witness testify against them, and listened as their lawyers tried to discredit each one. But there was no way of undoing the damage done by the girl who had been behind the bar at the Blind Beggar on 9 March, two years earlier. Despite her earlier statement that she had seen nothing that day, she now positively identified Ronnie Kray as the man who had blown George Cornell's brains out.

The twins were found guilty – Ronnie of the murder of George Cornell and Reggie of the killing of Jack McVitie and sentenced to life imprisonment, which the judge recommended should be a minimum of 30 years. They went down still protesting their innocence. Charlie was given ten years for being an accomplice.

Ronnie Kray died in a Slough hospital in 1995, having suffered a heart attack in prison, 27 years into his sentence. With a rather nice sense of irony, one of the hymns chosen to be sung at his funeral was 'Fight the Good Fight'. Reggie followed him to the grave five years later having been released on compassionate grounds, suffering from terminal cancer. Charles died the same year as Reggie – also of cancer and in jail where he was serving a ten-year sentence for his part in a £69 million cocaine smuggling plot.

The funerals of all three men brought the East End to a standstill. Their coffins were carried in a horse-drawn hearse. Countless cars followed the cortege. Crowds lined the streets. Flower shops in the area put their staff on overtime so great was the demand for wreaths and floral tributes. Some were from show business stars and personalities. Others came from ordinary East Enders who looked upon 'The Boys' with a curious mixture of fear and pride, and in some cases gratitude, for the Krays, Reggie especially, had been involved in charity work donating to old folks' homes, boys clubs and cancer appeals in their territory.

The Firm was not in the same league as the Mafia or the Cosa Nostra. Its criminal fiefdom was more akin to a bunch of 'jack the lads' than an evil, organized crime cartel. The Krays' career was startlingly improbable – three cockney villains who came close to establishing an empire of crime that showed just how out of touch the establishment was about the true scale of organized crime in Britain. 'Gangs like the Mafia, couldn't happen here,' was the attitude in the late 1950s and 1960s. The Krays came very close to making a nonsense of that mentality.

A Changing World

In the years following the Krays' arrest, Britain changed. The famously reserved British way of life went to the wind. It was out with the old and in with the new. In clubs and pubs all over the country soft drugs were, still are, openly used. The club culture with its throbbing music and almost hallucinogenic light displays seemed to encourage teenagers to slip an E – sometimes with tragic results.

In London, the old slums were being cleared to make way for more acceptable housing. What had been Kray and Richardson territory was colonized by 'Yuppies' who bought houses at a fraction of the price they would have to pay in Fulham, Chelsea and their other natural homes, and spend small fortunes renovating them. Many of the pubs where East End gangs had met and drunk were transformed into cocktail bars, with belly of pork in a mango jus replacing the packets of pork scratchings that had once hung behind the bar.

Many East Enders moved out to the new towns in nearby counties such as Essex (which police now reckon is the gangland capital of the United Kingdom) and Kent, and the suburbs of South London. Many had made the move much earlier: among them was Jim Noye, a one-time Bermondsey docker turned communications engineer. He settled in Bexleyheath and it was there, in 1947, that his son Kenny was born.

Britain's Public Enemy Number One

Kenny was a charming, hyperactive child – charming that is if you weren't on the receiving end of the protection racket he ran at Bexleyheath Secondary Modern School. When he left school he drifted into a life of crime and made a fortune at it. By the time he was thirty he was driving a Rolls Royce and had moved his wife, Brenda, and two sons into the peaceful Kent village of West Kingsdown, buying Hollywood Cottage, an imposing house surrounded by twenty acres of private land.

By the 1980s, he had appeared in court several times, on charges ranging from being found on enclosed premises for unlawful purposes to dishonestly abstracting electricity, from making false statements to the police to making false declarations to the VAT authorities.

But the police were well aware that these were trivial offences compared to the other crimes they suspected him of – laundering drug money, running a stolen motorcar parts ring and more. A police report of the early 1980s said that Noye allegedly put up

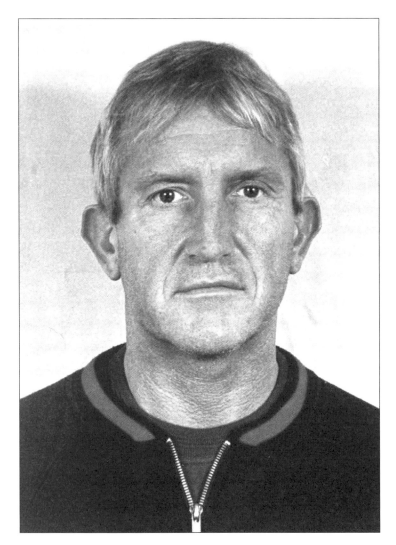

British gangland boss and road rage attacker Kenneth Noye.

the money for much organized crime in the south of England and was an associate of several prominent London criminals.

In 1983, a gang of men forced their way into a warehouse on the Heathrow International Trading Estate at Hounslow in West London and made off with £26 million of gold bullion from Unit 7. This was effectively a vast safe used by, amongst others, security company Brinks-Mat to store valuable cargoes of bullion, works of art, jewellery and other valuables. Police suspected an inside job and they were right. One of the guards who had been on duty,

Tony Black, was connected to a leading underworld gangster, Brian Robinson.

When confronted with what the police knew, Black confessed that he had supplied information to Robinson and that it had been he who had let the three-man gang into the warehouse. The other two were quickly identified and the three were eventually sent down for twenty-five years in prison.

The police had their men, or some of them, but there was still the matter of £26 million of bullion! Using their vast network of criminal contacts, they came up with a list of men they knew to be associates of the guilty men. Kenny Noye's name was on that list.

Months of investigation convinced the police that Noye was the most important link in a chain handling the stolen gold. From Noye, they concluded, it was passed down the chain, ending up with a bullion dealer in Bristol, Scadlynn.

The investigation had one tragic outcome. In January 1985, after Noye's house had been under surveillance for months, two policemen were sent into the grounds for close observation. They were scared off by three vicious-sounding Rottweilers. One of the men reached the road safely. When there was no sign of his colleague, DC John Fordham, two more policemen went to look. They found him lying on his back, Kenny Noye standing over him, shotgun in hand. Blood was oozing from a stab wound in Fordham's chest. He died shortly afterwards in hospital.

Noye was charged with John

Fordham's murder, but was later acquitted of the charge. He was not so lucky regarding his involvement in the Brinks-Mat robbery. A search of Hollywood Cottage revealed eleven gold bars worth £100,000 buried in a gully behind his garage wall.

The police investigation revealed that gold was passed from Noye to a friend called Brian Reader who in turn gave it Garth Chappell who re-smelted the gold, mixing it with copper to hide its purity. Scadlynn then sold it on the open market. Within six months, the gang had disposed of £13 million worth of gold bullion in this way.

For his part in the heist, Kenny Noye was fined £250,000 and jailed for thirteen years. He was out in 1994.

On his release, he decided to branch out into the comparatively new world of high-tech crime. Along with an old comrade-in-crime, John 'Little Legs' Lloyd, he formed what became known as 'The Hole in the Wall Gang'. Lloyd, it was well known throughout the underworld, was involved in the Brinks-Mat robbery but had never been brought to justice: when things had got too hot he had quite sensibly left the country for the United States.

He lived there on and off until 1994, often slipping back to Britain, despite the warrant out for his arrest. In that year he was named on the US TV crime show, *America's Most Wanted*, and decided things were getting too hot for him there.

Two weeks later, cool as the proverbial cucumber, he walked into London's Rochester Row police station and gave himself up, gam-

bling on the fact that none of the others arrested in connection with the Brinks-Mat raid, including his partner, Jean, would have split on him. The gamble paid off. The Crown Prosecution Service decided there was not enough evidence against him to bring a reasonable case to court.

Not long afterwards, in a pub just off London's Old Kent Road, popular with the city's criminal fraternity, Lloyd met up with Kenny Noye and some other known gangsters and told them he was planning a scam that would bring in a fortune. But before he could get the scheme off the ground, he needed backers.

Noye and the others agreed to put up the money and so 'The Hole in the Wall Gang' was formed. Its aim was to clone cash cards, which were to be used over a twenty-four-hour period to empty the accounts of thousands of innocent people all over the country. Never mind that these ordinary people would suffer, and never mind that the British banking system would be brought to its knees. There was, Lloyd estimated, around £100 million to be made.

The plan was to break into British Telecom exchanges and put a tap on telephone lines and memory boards. The information this yielded was to be used to clone a vast number of cash cards. To succeed, the gang needed to recruit corrupt communications and computer experts.

First on the gang's shopping list was a criminal computer geek. One of the gang, Paul Kidd, knew just the person. Kidd owned a legitimate van hire business as well as having a finger in many criminal pies. In a gesture to show just what a good citizen he was, Kidd offered to take convicts from open prisons, who were allowed out to retrain for their release. One of the men Kidd gave this opportunity to was Martin Grant, who was serving a sentence for attempted murder. While inside he had studied for a degree in electronic communication.

When Kidd heard this, he told the gang had just the man they needed. Grant agreed but soon became terrified of the gang, especially Noye and Lloyd who were looked upon as gods by his fellow prisoners. At one meeting, the two men produced details of Grant's family background that had clearly been given to them by bent prison authorities. And when on one of his days out, Lloyd drove Grant to his (Grant's) mother's house in his words, 'just to let me know he knew where she lived,' Grant went to the police and talked. The police were so worried at what would happen to Grant if the gang realized he had talked, that they had him under twenty-four-hour armed protection.

Lloyd was sentenced to five years' imprisonment, He was released in 1999 and has kept a low profile ever since. When the police moved in to arrest Noye he was nowhere to be seen.

In May 1996, he knifed to death an innocent man called Stephen Cameron, in a road-rage attack in the Kent section of the M25. Noye fled the country but was back a few months later, moving from safe house to safe house. And such was his power that he could drink quite openly in his old haunts knowing that no one would 'grass' on him.

In 1997 he moved to a small village in southern Spain from where he is alleged to have made drugs deals worth millions of pounds. He needed the money: he reckoned he was spending around £50,000 a month just to keep one step ahead of the law. He travelled abroad using false passports to go through immigration controls. He visited Yardie bosses in Jamaica to do business with them. He sailed to Gibraltar on his yacht to meet with a local drugs baron. He even hired the yacht out to drug smugglers.

He did all this even though the police in several countries were looking for him. He managed to bring his father and wife out to Spain to visit him, even though the Kent police were meant to be watching their every move, hoping they would lead them to Noye. And on one occasion, more than a dozen Spanish policemen patrolled the grounds of the house next door to his where one of Spain's leading politicians was staying, unaware that Britain's most wanted man was lounging by the pool across the wall.

But in August 1998, thanks to a tip-off, the Kent police traced Kenny Noye to his house in Atlanterra, a tiny village on the coast just south of Cadiz. He was arrested and the extradition process began. At first his lawyers were confident they would succeed in fighting deportation to Britain, but ten moths after his arrest, two last-ditch appeals failed, and Noye was taken from his cell in Madrid's Valdemoro Jail and put on a plane for London's Gatwick Airport.

Illegal immigrants from Afghanistan gather at night to board a passing freight train March 18, 2002 at the Channel Tunnel Freight terminal in Frethun, France. Taken from Afghanistan by "people smugglers", they have paid between eight and 12,000 dollars to be transported across eastern Europe to France.

While awaiting trial for the murder of Stephen Cameron he was held at London's most secure prison, Belmarsh, where according to one inmate he was treated like a king. Before his trial began, the judge ordered round-the-clock protection for each juror. His claim of self-defence fell on deaf ears (at least, eleven out of twelve deaf ears) and he was sentenced to life imprisonment.

Today, the man who was Britain's Number One Gangster is now in Whitemoor prison. It's a top-security jail, but even so it's more than likely that Kenny Noye is still in contact with his old partners in crime, planning for the day when he is eventually released and for the day when he will reclaim his place at the top of the gangland tree.

New kids on the block

Gangland UK has changed. The old-style criminals of the 1950s and '60s were a different kettle of fish from the organized criminals of today. Fifty years ago, many of the big time gangsters were rotten to the core, but curiously that had a stablizing influence on the communities they lived in. They inspired respect, not just among rival gangsters, but among the small-time petty mobsters who otherwise might have been tempted to prey on people in the territory ruled by one of the big gangs. In South London, for instance, the Richardson gang ruled with a rod of iron, but some policemen reckon this had a beneficial effect on small-time crime. 'No one would dare rob an old lady's sweetie shop on their manor,' one ex-policeman said.

These and other gangsters of the time, men like the Krays, enjoyed publicity and loved nothing better than to hobnob with sport personalities and film stars. Today's gangsters, men like Kenny Noye, 'Little Legs' Lloyd, 'Cocky Warren' and others, are shadowy figures, whose names are unknown to most of us until they are caught and come to trial.

And whereas not so long ago guns were a rarity, they are now, despite Britain's stringent gun laws, carried as a matter of course by big-time and small-time criminals alike. The number of gun crimes has rocketed in recent years and now hardly a day goes by without the report of a shooting in some part of the country. Guns can be bought for as little as £500 and rented for even less.

The crimes have changed, too. In the old days gangs ran prostitution, extortion rackets, illegal gambling and other scams, but they didn't affect the ordinary man in the street.

Today's organized crimes are different. For example, forgery is big time business: Barclays Bank reckons that at any one time there is around £200 million in counterfeit currency in circulation. There's money in illegal immigrants and credit card fraud. But it is in drugs that the real money is to be made.

More heroin was seized in 2000 in Britain than in any other European country. Opium floods into the UK at an ever-increasing rate, and although Customs seize more than a ton of cocaine every year, that's it only a fraction of what gets through. And

Bridge Park Sports Centre, Wembley, scene of a horrific gangland execution after a negligent council employed a Yardie crime boss to run security.

with the profits to be made, that's no wonder.

A kilo of cocaine bought 'whole-sale' from one of the Colombian cartels costs around £1,500. Cut and sold in the clubs and streets of Britain's cities, the same weight brings in more than £100,000. Ecstasy, bought in Holland for £6 a tablet, sells in some London clubs for four times that amount.

Cannabis, which is still illegal in the UK but which is increasingly tolerated by the police, is bought in the West Indies where it costs £100 a kilo. The street price in London makes the same kilo worth £2,000.

Central to drug dealing in the UK, particularly in London, are the Yardies. The term is a moniker given by Jamaican people themselves to someone who has recently arrived in the UK from Jamaica, which is referred to as 'the back yard'.

The Yardies in Britain

The present-day influence of the Yardies in the UK has its genesis in the economic climate of the post-war years. During the 1950s, Britain enjoyed an economic boom.

The expression 'You've never had it so good' seemed to sum up the times. There was employment for everybody: in fact, there were not enough people to fill all the jobs either on offer or that it was envisaged would be created in the future. Consequently the British government encouraged immigration to fill the vacancies, and as a result

*Passers-by come to the aid of shooting victim, South London. The murder rate in the UK
capital is soaring, due in large part to the increasing incidence of gang-related killings.*

many Afro-Caribbeans from Jamaica came to Britain in search of a better standard of living.

They were mostly unskilled but hard working people who often found themselves living in run-down inner city areas. When the country's economic fortunes changed and recession set in, many of the people in this new workforce were first to feel the pinch. This left many of the Jamaicans, especially second-generation ones, finding it difficult to match what they could achieve with what they wanted to achieve.

By the mid-1960s, within these low-income communities, some people had turned to crime, just as immigrant families in the US who, like their UK counterparts, live in

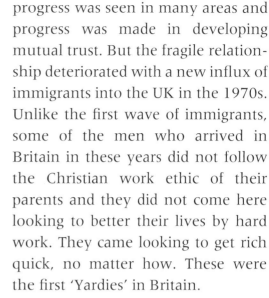

progress was seen in many areas and progress was made in developing mutual trust. But the fragile relationship deteriorated with a new influx of immigrants into the UK in the 1970s. Unlike the first wave of immigrants, some of the men who arrived in Britain in these years did not follow the Christian work ethic of their parents and they did not come here looking to better their lives by hard work. They came looking to get rich quick, no matter how. These were the first 'Yardies' in Britain.

The UK was attractive to the Yardies because of its long-standing association with its former colonies in the Caribbean. They share a common language (or the basis of a common language) and several cultural, social, sporting and religious values – factors upon which legitimate immigration is based

Once in the UK, the Yardies became involved in the drug scene, making sales at first mainly within their own communities and at first mainly marijuana. But they have moved on, and now supply cocaine and crack cocaine, which they get from the Cali cartel, to anyone with the money to pay for them. Paying to feed a drug habit, police in London estimate, is now responsible for much of the street crime and house break-ins that take place in the capital each year.

Yardies compete with Turkish gangs for control of the heroin market. Scotland Yard reckon that London's Turkish gangs have links to Turkish organized crime, and may be involved in terrorism. And along with the drugs they smuggle in (from Afghanistan into Turkey and from

cheap, poor-quality, often public housing, often did. These communities house a disproportionate number of the unemployed, and the estates a disproportionately high rate of violence and drug-related crime.

Over the years, police relations with the communities became strained and sometimes violently confrontational. But considerable there up through Europe into Britain from Holland and Belgium), they bring in countless illegal immigrants. Estimates of their turnover range from £8 billion upwards.

Shootings within Turkish gangland have counted for at least 20 fatal shootings in the capital since the new millennium. They are also increasingly common within the Yardie community.

Yardies are, according to police records, generally single males between the ages of 18 and 35. They are usually unemployed, although when challenged some claim to be working 'in the music business' or 'doing the clubs'. They often enter the country as tourists or to 'visit relatives', sometimes on false passports. Once in the UK they assume false identities and carry forged credentials.

'Yardie' crime in the UK has no 'Mr Bigs' as the Mafia and other organized-crime syndicates do. There is no pyramid of ranks as there is in the Cosa Nostra. 'Yardie' groups have a relatively, small, flat organization structure. The rise to the top is a relatively short step for anyone with access to drugs and a willingness to use force and guns. In many cases, the 'top man' not only imports drugs, but is personally involved in street dealing.

There are occasional conflicts between Yardie gangs, but nothing on the same scale as the internecine disputes that have spilled blood on the streets of Palermo and New York. In fact, the gangs are often mutually supportive and being a member of one is no bar to belonging to another. The gangs frequently break up and re-organize, although the more stable ones, like their big brothers in other longer established criminal organizations, are now starting to establish straight businesses as fronts for their illegal activities and as a way of laundering the proceeds. Unlike them, though, there is little evidence that they have 'bought' policemen to turn a blind eye, or to see that if they are arrested, evidence is not available and charges are dropped.

But what they do have in common with all other gangs, with the likes of Kenny Noye and his fellow UK gangsters, with the Turkish gangs and others, is a belief that they are above the law.

That's not just Gangland UK; it's Gangland the world over.

This belief shared by members of criminal gangs and street gangs is one of the factors behind the increasing use of firearms as rival gangs square up to each other in their various turf wars. These disputes over territories, revenge for supposed slights or for injuries inflicted by members of one gang on members of another have seen scores of people shot dead in the streets of Britain's cities, especially London, in the last decade.

It used to be the Jamaican Yardies who were to blame for much of the capital's violent crime, but today British-born youths are at the forefront of gangland gun culture, something that is spreading across the country.

According to the Metropolitan Police Deputy Assistant Commissioner, Mike Fuller, who heads Operation Trident, the Met's initiative against drug-related violent crime, many of the youths who would once have been regarded as 'Yardies' now refer to themselves as 'Crews' and 'Posses'.

He says that while there are still some Jamaicans involved in London's gang culture, much of the 'gang crime' the Met is now seeing is the result of conflicts between rival gangs of British-born black youths. He insists that this is in no way a racist view: it is one backed up by Home Office statistics. He is also backed up in this by the fact that there are several cases of British-born black gangs expanding their operations and travelling to Jamaica to commit crimes – armed robbery, drug dealing, assault and attempted murder – there.

In London and other metropolitan areas, there is a new generation of young guns, almost all under twenty-five, who have modelled themselves on the original Yardies and are now their equal in brutality, cold-bloodedness and sheer bravado. Gun shots are now fired almost daily in the capital, where inter-gang disputes that would once have been settled by fists (or knives at the worst) are now settled by the bullet.

In August 2001, a nineteen-year-old youth was dragged from his car after being chased by members of a rival gang through west London, pistol-whipped about the head and shot in the leg. It was no isolated incident. In the two weeks that followed, a twenty-year-old man went on a shooting rampage in the West End after an argument with a bouncer in a nightclub. In the days that followed, a man was shot dead as he sat on a wall in East London,

another met a similar fate at the hands of two gunmen on a motor bike as he walked through Pickett's Lock, not far away. And only a few hours later another was shot in the leg, in Brixton, an area of South London long connected with drug pushing and street gang culture.

It is not just on the streets where the use of guns by young gang members has been seen. In the months before these incidents, a car outside a primary school was sprayed with bullets from an automatic gun, a deputy headmaster was pistol-whipped in his own school's dining room, and children as young as fourteen were reported to have been seen carrying weapons in broad daylight on the streets of Harlesden in North London.

According to a social worker on a notorious housing estate in the area, teenagers don't talk about beating up the members of another gang for some actual or supposed slight, they talk about killing each other:

'The simple fact is that with a gun you are someone; you can hold your own. Without one, you are a dead man. The kids who end up getting involved in the gang scene are often growing up in fatherless homes with no role models apart from the flashy image of local gangsters who flaunt their expensive cars and gold jewellery with pride. They feel that the only way they will ever get something for themselves is to copy them. Once that decision has been made, however subconsciously, it's a short step to drug dealing and running with the gang in charge of it in their area.'

The mother of the victim of a gang/drug related murder insisted her son wasn't a gangster, after his body was found floating in a London canal with four bullets in his head, in August 2000. 'He was just an ordinary kid. He got into selling drugs because everyone here gets into selling drugs,' she sobbed. 'I pleaded with him to stop but he just didn't listen.'

London remains the centre of black-on-black inter-gang violence, but the problem is rapidly spreading to other parts of the country. Gangs in cities outside London are often led by men who were once Jamaican Yardies but who feel unable to compete in the capital. In Birmingham, for example, in the first year of the new millennium there more than fifty shootings, several murders, drive-by shootings and woundings, all of which were blamed by the police on the turf wars between existing gangs and newcomers threatening to muscle in on their territories and operations.

Even the cobbled streets of sedate Edinburgh are not immune to gangland violence, most of it fuelled by drugs. In July 2001, the two key players in a gang trying to profit from increasing the sales of crack cocaine in the city. In 1999 there were four seizures of the cocaine derivative in all of Scotland: in the first six months of the following year, there were thirty-four.

All over the United Kingdom, gangs are becoming more organized, more sophisticated and more willing to use guns, not as a last resort but as a first one. 'We are not talking about levels of organization or violence on a par with Los Angeles,' said a senior London policeman in the summer of 2001. 'But these people [gangs] should not be underestimated. And whereas it used to be that the only victims of gangland and inter-gang violence were gang members, with the widespread acceptance of firearms as the norm, the potential for innocent bystanders to get caught in the crossfire is always there.'

GANGLAND USA

THE United States is the largest economy in the world. Where there is such widespread activity there is money to be made. Where there is money to be made, there is crime. And where there is crime there are gangs, the most famous of which is the Mafia – the network of 'Families' that once ran crime coast to coast in the country.

Between 1980 and 2000 the FBI spearheaded a massive assault on the Cosa Nostra. It put enormous pressure on the unions that were controlled by the Mafia, and considerably reduced the Cosa Nostra's financial and political power in the process. It also mounted a huge intelligence-gathering operation in cooperation with state and local police. Together with widespread use of anti-organized-crime legislation these measures crippled many of the Mafia families and hundreds of smaller gangs.

By the turn of the millennium many Mafia racketeers such as John Gotti, Vincent Gigante, John Riggo and Andrew Russo had been convicted and sentenced to long prison sentences. Indeed there were

so many successful convictions that New York's Mayor Rudy Giuliani predicted that the day would come when the city's major crime families would soon be reduced to little more than street gangs.

But, as the *New York Times* wrote, 'Although prosecutors portrayed the indictments as a triumphant blow to organized crime, the allegations also testified to the resilience of the Mafia. Despite repeated indictments it has been able to continue to hold its lucrative ventures and enter into new ones like telecommunications fraud.'

The article went on to say that while the Mafia families had lost clout in many of the areas in which they operated – the fish and construction industries, garbage collection and the garment industry, or instance – the mainstays of loan-sharking, gambling and brothel keeping still keep the money rolling in.

Mafia men behind bars still wield considerable power from their prison cells. They have huge funds at their disposal, and even in the dog-eat-dog twenty-first century, the Mafia family code of honour is still a force to be reckoned with.

Meanwhile, outside the prisons, a new breed of Mafia men is focusing on lucrative white-collar crimes such as stock swindles, the sale of pre-paid telephone cards, and mobile phone and medical insurance frauds.

'The Families are in transition' said Lewis D. Schiliro, the head of the FBI's New York office. 'They're trying to figure out how to redirect their criminal activities in a new environment.'

And so, in the middle of the first decade of the twenty-first century, more than a hundred years since Italians started to migrate in large numbers from Sicily, heading for the USA, and despite the massive efforts of the authorities, Cosa Nostra families continue to operate in New York and Chicago. They adapt to changing times and the new tactics the law-enforcement agencies use against them, not just in these two cities, but in other ones, coast to coast, too.

Hell's Angels

On 4 July 1948, four thousand motorcyclists, many of them disaffected World War Two veterans, roared into the small town of Hollister, south of Oakland, California. By the time they left, fifty bikers had been injured and over one hundred of them were in jail. The Hell's Angels had been born.

Its leading light was Sonny Barger. Founder of the Oakland Chapter, Barger is credited with turning what was a bunch of dissolute, disorganized and wild bike riders into the organization it is today. Fuelled

by films such as the 1952 biker movie, *The Wild One*, starring Marlon Brando, more and more bikers flocked to join. Within a few years there were chapters of the Hell's Angels not just in towns and cities coast to coast in the US, but in Europe and the other continents of the world.

In the early days there was talk of nauseating initiation ceremonies involving sodomy, group sex and defecation. There was wild suggestions of some chapters demanding that before a candidate was admitted to membership they had to have sex in front of witnesses first with an under-age girl, then with a woman aged sixty-five or older, and finally with a corpse. And even wilder, one chapter was said to demand that would-be members prove they had committed a murder before they were allowed in.

All nonsense of course, but rumours like these fuelled the Angels' reputation as the wild bunch. When the members of one chapter or other arrived in town, people pulled their blinds down and locked up their daughters.

In 1966, the Angels, guided by Barger, legally incorporated themselves, issuing five hundred shares and in their articles of association declaring that they existed for 'the promotion and advancement of motorcycle riding, motorcycle clubs, motorcycle highway safety and all phases of motorcycles and motorcycle driving'. The flying death's head that had become the gang's unofficial symbol was patented in 1972, and since then the various chapters that

Hells Angel Ralph "Sonny" Barger appears at a book signing July 18, 2001 in Milan, Italy. (Photo by Mario Magnani/Getty Images)

compose the gang have vigorously defended their copyright in the symbol.

The Hell's Angels inspired other biker gangs – the Sons of Satan, the Pagans, and Satan's Slaves, for example. They all contrived to look much the same – leather jackets painted with garish symbols, often Nazi in origin; helmets similarly adorned, the wearers' long, lank hair streaming out from underneath. In

Group of Hell's Angels attending 55th Annual 4th of July Weekend Event, commemorating the 1947 incident when outlaw motorcyclists supposedly overran the town of Hollister. (Photo by Chuck Nacke/Timepix/Time Life Pictures/Getty Images)

the 1990s there was a move to smarten up the image. Some chapters abandoned the uniforms of earlier members in favour of sharp suits and neat haircuts. And in a bid to give their image a boost, the Vancouver Chapter rode through the city streets bearing Christmas presents for poor children of the city.

The Angels and drugs

The majority of the Angels' activities are crime-free (unless the decibel level reached by several hundred bikes at full rev is to be considered a crime), but there is an inner core that is involved in drug trafficking and other misdemeanours. In Europe, biker gangs eschew their motorcycles and take to BMWs and Mercedes to smuggle drugs across national borders. Scotland Yard reckon that the bike gangs' involvement in drugs smuggling is one of the fastest-growing areas of crime.

Official investigations have uncovered evidence of links between drugs cartels in the United States and bike gangs in Europe; the drugs, mainly cocaine, being brought into Europe via ports in Spain and Portugal and distributed by the gangs throughout the continent. This activity is believed to be co-ordinated by a 'legitimate' enterprise that binds various European chapters together in a legal framework, but which is also thought to be a highly efficient money-laundering operation.

In the United States, the Hell's Angels started to manufacture amphetamines in the 1960s to fund legal costs. Today, they are thought to

control the market there and some chapters have probably moved on to operate other rackets. One expert in gang culture in the States has gone so far as to write that the bike gangs are on the point of overtaking the Mafia as the leading street-crime organization – supplying drugs and firearms, running prostitutes and other vice rackets – if they haven't already done so. As one senior North American police officer said in the 1990s, 'The Angels are the new kids on the block. In forty years they have done what it took the Cosa Nostra a century to achieve.'

Street gangs

Street gangs are nothing new in the United States or anywhere else in the world. They have probably existed since villages started to develop into towns, towns grow into cities, and gangs of youths formed to defend their patch of territory. At some point in history, unscrupulous politicians realized that these gangs had their uses and began to exploit them to help them enforce their views and get their own ways.

Many major Mafia figures first drew blood in the street gangs of New York that ran wild in the city in the early years of the last century. Among them was the James Street Gang, which spawned John Torrio, one of the most notorious gangsters of all time, and the Jimmy Curly Gang. The latter operated along 59th Street in New York from 1910 until the US entered World War One. It had about twenty members, specializing in extortion, kidnapping and contract killings. In 1914 it fought the rival Gas House Gang for control of the street, and in the shoot-out that followed, six men ended up in hospital with gunshot wounds and the Gas House Gang's leader was taken by cart to the city morgue.

In the 1920s it is reckoned that there were around one thousand three hundred street gangs in Chicago alone, many sponsored by local politicians and businessmen. Among these gangs were the Colts, originally known as the Morgan Athletic Club. In the early years of the twentieth century, its members, usually the sons of Irish stockyard workers, were recruited by the two brothers who ran one of the city's newspapers. At the street level, the younger members were paid to beat up newspaper boys delivering a rival newspaper owned by the legendary William Randolph Hearst and his partner.

The club, whose motto was 'Hit me and you hit two thousand', was taken over in 1908 by Frank Ragen, one of

Early New York street gang the Gophers pose for this rare photograph, taken in the later 1890s.

the Democratic commissioners for the city's Cook County. The name was changed to the Ragen Athletic Club, and became known as the Ragen Colts. They did feature in the city's amateur baseball league, but it was not for their sporting prowess that the gang is remembered. Ragen paid the rent on their premises and other expenses in exchange for their services in intimidating his political opponents. Gang members were also paid to ensure that black citizens kept to their own areas.

The Ragen Athletic Club played a major part in the race riots that rocked the city in the summer of 1919, after some black teenagers went for a swim and had the cheek to come ashore on a 'white only' beach. The boys were showered with rocks thrown by Ragen gang members, and one of the swimmers drowned as a result. In the ensuing riots thirty-six people (twenty-two of them black) were killed and more than five hundred injured.

In the outcry that followed, the Colts' club charter was revoked, but things were soon back to normal, although Ragen changed his sponsorship to the Sheldon gang and backed the activities of a newcomer to town – Al Capone. The Colts disbanded, some of its members getting involved in bootlegging and other criminal activities; others went on to found the Chicago Maroons, who later as the Chicago Cardinals became a team to be reckoned with in the National Football League.

On the west coast, there have been Hispanic gangs from the turn of the twentieth century when Mexican refugees from the country's political troubles settled in city suburbs of southwestern cities, suburbs that they made their own. Today, many of the modern Spanish-speaking gangs can trace their ancestry back to the factions formed during the Mexican Revolution.

The first of the Los Angeles Afro-American gangs were the Good-fellows, the Magnificents (from the east side of the city), the Driver Brothers, the Blodgettes and the Boozies, the last of which was heavily into robbery and prostitution.

By the time the United States entered World War Two, these gangs had faded. They were replaced by the Purple Hearts and other gangs that took their names from the streets or areas they controlled. The years after the War came to an end saw an expansion in black street gang activity.

In 1965, street riots broke out in the Watts district of the city. Following the example of black gang members, rioters rampaged through the streets, looting and burning. Similar riots occurred in the black ghettos of other US cities such as Chicago and Detroit. When peace was eventually restored, many of the gangs disbanded: others turned to black-power politics.

In 1980, a federal survey concluded that there were ten US cities with serious street gang problems. Within ten years, this number had risen to a hundred and twenty-five, the worst of them being in the midwest and west. Chicago was thought to have one hundred and twenty-five gangs, with twelve

'Turn left or get shot' a sign warns drivers in the Watts area of Los Angeles during the race riots of 1965.

thousand members between them. In New York, surprisingly, there were supposed to be just a thousand members in the few gangs that ran the streets. At the other side of the country, Los Angeles was seen to be the gang capital of the country.

In 1995, the US Department of Justice reported that eight out of every ten cities with a population of over a hundred thousand had significant street gang activity. By then, two of the LA gangs, the Crips and the Bloods, had started to establish their presence in all the 'mainland' states of the Union.

The Crips were founded in 1971 by Stanley 'Tookie' Williams and Raymond Lee Washington to 'provide protection' in their neighbourhood. The protection they offered usually ran to a promise not to steal dinner money from fellow students at their high school in exchange for a share of it.

Washington had already founded a gang, the Baby Avenues, a junior branch of the city's Avenue gang. 'You should be in your cribs,' said one Avenue member when he heard of the fledgling gang, and it became known as the Avenue Cribs.

According to one version, when Washington and Williams joined forces 'Cribs' became corrupted into 'Crips': another version is that it took its name from the horror film, *Tales of the Crypt.* A third has it that one of the original members was handicapped and in his honour the others shortened the word 'cripple' to 'crips'. A fourth version is that when the first members were looking for a name, they wanted something that summed up the hard, tough image they wanted to project. The hardest, toughest substance they could think of was Kryptonite, the only thing that could harm Superman. And Kryptonite became Crips.

Whichever is true, within a few months, other LA gangs were incorporated into the Crips, some voluntarily, others being forced into association. Feuding between the two factions often led to violence, as happened in 1972 when two allied Crips gangs attacked a rival one called the Piru Street Boys. Heavily outnumbered, the Piru Street Boys were defeated, but rather than let themselves be absorbed into the Crips, they turned to other LA gangs for help. As a result a rival organization to the Crips – the Bloods – was born. By the early 1980s the Crips and the Bloods between them could muster somewhere in the region of fifteen thousand members.

The two rivals looked to other more established gangs like Chicago's Folks for inspiration. From them they developed their philosophy of 'all for one and one for all' and a demand of lifetime devotion to the gang's mores. Following their example, they introduced strict rules of conduct and clothing codes. Anyone who violates the rules is disciplined according to the gang's rules. Punishments range from performing menial tasks for other members, to being physically beaten and even, in extreme cases, to being killed.

The Crips wear blue clothes to identify themselves to other members and to set them apart from other gangs. The blue is often blended with

Members of the Crips street gang show off their hardware, Compton.

black, brown and purple. Red is the colour of the Bloods, although other colours can be used if they have a special significance to a particular gang. For example, the Lime Street Pirus often wear green. The colours are seen especially in accessories such as headgear, handkerchiefs, shoe-laces and belts. Gang members also use jewellery and hand signalling to communicate with each other.

Members of both gangs often call each other 'cuz' – short for 'cousin'. They also identify each other by a nickname or 'moniker', which is often the only name by which one member is known to another. Often, the first letter of the real name is used to prefix the gang moniker. Thus a young man called Charles who wants to present an image that is as hard as nails may style himself 'C-Nails'.

Hatred of one gang for the other is often so intense that if possible Bloods change the first letter of a word starting with a 'C' to a 'B'. Similarly, Crips will change a 'B 'at the start of a word to a 'C'. Thus, in Blood terms 'cigarette; becomes 'bigarette' and in Crips' terminology 'brown' may become 'crown'. Childish, certainly. But there is nothing childish about the gangs' activities – automobile theft, drugs trafficking, rape and violence.

Both gangs use graffiti to com-municate territorial limits, to broadcast warnings and to publicize challenges to other street gangs.

Neither of the gangs has centralized leadership. The structure is frag-mented, something that makes it difficult for the police to keep track of them. Individual gangs are called 'sets', each of which is affiliated to the others within a specified geographical area. For example, the Compton Crips are made up of more than twenty individual sets, each one con-trolling a small part of the Compton's territory. In Los Angeles there are thought to be two hundred Crips sets and around seventy Bloods ones.

Within each set there are usually four distinct types of members. Hard-core members are just that. They talk gang, act gang and dress gang. These are the members who are at the criminal heart of the gang – the drug pushers, petty thieves and maybe pimps.

'Associates' identify with a set within its neighbourhood, but sel-dom involve themselves other than marginally with gang activity, per-haps using then as dope suppliers.

'Peripherals' are non-gang members, often women, who identi-fy with a gang and use it for protection in return for favours such as carrying drugs or guns.

The last type of gang member is the 'Wannabe', kids who claim to be members of a set in another part of town, for the kudos they think this brings them. They wear the set's colours and use their slang.

Most gang members are between fifteen and thirty-five, the members at the younger end of the range tending to be those most ready to use violence in an attempt to raise their status within the gang. There is usually at least one 'Old Gangster' – a hard core and often a founder member in each gang. At the bottom end of the scale are the 'BGs' or 'TGs' – 'baby gangsters' and 'tiny gangsters' respectively whose activities are usually controlled by 'shot callers' – older members who have earned their reputations.

Recruitment is usually from the 'Wannabes' and is often aggressively pursued. Recruits have to prove that they have a 'knowledge' of the gang's history, dress code, graffiti and activities. Would-be members must prove their loyalty to the gang and may be asked to commit a crime, attack someone outside the gang or run some sort of risk to prove that they would lay down their lives for the gang.

New recruits usually have to undergo an initiation ceremony such as 'Walking the Line'. This involves the prospective initiate, hands tied behind his back, walking between two lines of gang members who kick and beat him in an effort to bring the recruit to his knees. If they succeed, it's back to the beginning again.

Would-be Bloods must spill blood, either their own or someone else's, before they are accepted into the gang. Once in, they are often tattooed with the set's symbol. For example, the New York Bloods, who refer to each other as 'dogs', are tattooed with two dots over a single one to represent a dog's paw.

The United States street gang culture is one of the most extraordinary social phenomena of the last forty or so years. The Crips and the Bloods have sets in cites all over the country. They are not the only gangs, of course. In Chicago the Black Gangster Discipline Nation or

Graffiti advocating an end to inter-gang violence between the Bloods and the Crips, and a united assault on the police (187 is the LAPD code for 'Officer in trouble').

Gangster Disciples (Folk) was set up as a challenge to the Black P Stone Nation (People) gang which evolved from the 1960s Blackstone Rangers. Gangs all over the United States claim allegiance to one or other of the Chicago gangs. When the Folk's leader Larry 'King' Hoover was sentenced to one hundred and twenty-five years in jail for the murder of a gang member suspected of stealing drugs, he continued to run the gang from inside his various cells, through his wife who turned Folk merchandizing into a profitable sideline.

'They are the family'

Why are so many young people attracted to life in one or other of the street gangs? One Chicago judge believes it's because they have no families to nourish them, or that their parents are as socially dysfunctional as their street-wide children. Another judge backed this opinion, saying that the family unit has been replaced by gangs. 'They are the family. Once they would say, "Don't talk that way about my parents." Now it's "Don't talk that way about the gang."' He went on to point out that whereas some law-abiding youngsters work for McDonald's, say, for $4 an hour, others are making a hundred times more than from drug running and street crime.

'These kids [the gang members] know kids their own age who are dead. They have no sense of future. Their future is now and they go for it with gusto!'

Asian Street Gangs

Vietnamese, Laotian and Cambodian gangs represent the bulk of Asian criminal street activity in the USA, especially in California where there are substantial communities of Southeast Asian immigrants. It was in the 1970s that the Vietnamese gangs began to make their presence felt on the streets, followed by Laotian and Cambodian ones in the 1980s. The gangs ranged in size from five to two hundred members, their crimes mainly residential and business burglaries and car theft. They were rarely involved in the violent, retaliatory drive-by shootings that were the hallmark of some of their white counterparts. Their ages ranged from fifteen to twenty-five, with the older members usually donning the mantle of leadership, surrendering it to younger members when they were either jailed for their various misdemeanours or drifted away from the gang.

The early Asian gangs were loose-knit, with members associating with each other on a non-continuous basis. Members moved from gang to gang and, to begin with, they had none of the tattoos, graffiti, hand signs or other characteristics that other gangs used to set themselves apart from their rivals. Indeed these Asian gangs had no names and no turf.

By 1985, the Vietnamese gangs had turned to organized car theft, extortion, gun crimes, witness intimidation, assault and murder. Rather than prey on the affluent white suburbs, they began to target Vietnamese communities, ruthlessly and viciously, gangs from one city travelling to another to commit their crimes. Gradually, they and the other Asian gangs became more formal in structure and became turf-oriented – something that brought with it the violence of the turf wars common among other gangs. Today, there is an increasing use of hallmark clothing, tattoos, graffiti and other symbols that set the members of one gang apart from those of another. There are reckoned to be around 15,000 Asian gangs operating in California alone, with at least double that number in the rest of the country. Members range in age from thirteen to thirty-five.

White Street Gangs

Post-war street gangs in the US were often oriented around motorcycle gangs like the Hell's Angels. Today, such bike gangs are considered by the US authorities as organized crime groups rather than street gangs, the most important among the latter being the Skinheads.

As with so many US social phenomena, it was in California that Skinheads were first seen to surface as a major problem. It was there, in the late 1980s, that they were initially identified as the primary source of white street gang violence and in the decades that have followed, Skinhead gangs have spread from coast to coast.

Characterized by their shaven heads and their philosophy of white supremacy, Skinhead groups were formed as racist gangs and were neither turf-oriented nor profit-

motivated. Their crimes ranged from vandalism to assault, sometimes murder, and they targeted their activities against non-whites, Jews, the homeless and homosexuals.

Racist skinhead band Skrewdriver wow their somewhat diminutive audience.

Random assault was their norm.

Skinhead gangs drew their numbers from disaffected teenagers and young adults, both male and female. Their weapons included baseball bats, knives and steel-toed boots; only occasionally did a Skinhead carry a gun.

It was not long after they made their appearance on the streets of the United States that they were seen to be using graffiti, hand signs and tattoos for the same purposes as other gangs. Among their graffito are swastikas and lightning bolts, but whereas other gangs use graffiti to mark their territories, Skinheads use it to deface their victims' property. Hand signs include the Nazi salute and using fingers to form the letters 'W' and 'P' – White Power. Their tattoos include the swastika, the Nazi flag, hooded Ku Klux Klansmen and the letters 'SWP' (Supreme White Power) and 'WAR' (White Aryan Resistance).

Shortly after Skinheads were identified as an increasing presence on the streets, the US authorities were alarmed (but not surprised) to learn that they were beginning to establish associations with more traditional white supremacy groups. Gang members were known to have attended KKK and WAR rallies, marches and demonstrations, and have participated in cross-burning ceremonies.

In 1988, Skinheads in Oregon were convicted of the murder of an Ethiopian immigrant, beating him to death with a baseball bat, and since then their continued associations with violent white supremacist groups have been viewed with increasing alarm by the US authorities.

They remain a loose-knit and comparatively unorganized group, but in the past few years there is evidence that several of the gangs have developed an internal gang structure. Some have printed and distributed membership application forms, collected subscriptions and established rules and regulations for their members. Some have even been known to take formal minutes of their meetings.

Unlike most other street gangs, Skinheads are not territorial and are not inspired to commit crimes for profit, and although they are not the most numerous of the white street gangs, they are the most violent. Their potential for igniting the often tinderbox-dry relationships between disaffected young blacks and poor white communities is a constant worry to US Police Departments.

The Gang Look

Parents, not just in the US but in many other countries, are often dismayed when their teenage children come home from a shopping trip sporting 'the gangbanger' look – baggy jeans, hooded sweatshirts, the latest expensive trainers or whatever the current style of the streets demands. They instantly assume that their children have joined a gang and brace themselves for what lies in store. They (at least most of them) need not worry. Street gang membership, although growing, is restricted to a comparative few. All their children are doing is doing what children have been doing since time immemorial – cocking a snook at authority. And what better way to do it than to wear clothes of which authority obviously disapproves?

Prison gangs

Probably for as long as society has sent its criminals to prison, there have been prison gangs. But it is generally accepted that the first modern US prison gang came about when young Mexicans in the Deuel Vocational Institute in Tracey, California, banded together to protect themselves from attack from non-Hispanic inmates. That was in 1957. Within a year or two, the gang, who styled themselves 'Eme', 'The Mexican Mafia', or 'The MM', was controlling homosexual prostitution, gambling and drug distribution within the prison. Violence was the gang's trademark. Membership was often restricted to those who had assaulted (even killed) a prison officer or fellow inmate.

As members were transferred to other jails, they took their Mexican Mafia ways with them. New members were recruited from convicts who had been leaders of street gangs on the outside. By 1984 Eme had challenged the Italian and Jewish prison gangs who had 'controlled things' in many US prisons for decades, and had become one of the four most powerful of the gangs. By the end of the 1980s, members who had served their sentences took their Eme loyalties with them into the world outside and started dealing in drugs on the street, while their amigos still controlled the drug trade inside.

Their main rivals were (still are) a Mexican-American gang known as 'La Nuestra Familia'. It was formed in the 1960s to offer protection to prisoners under threat from Eme members. It wasn't long before it moved into the same rackets as the MM and when La Nuestra Familia started to challenge the MM's pre-eminence in the heroin trade in US jails, things got nasty. Within five or six years, thirty prisoners had been killed in the inter-gang war that was being fought in US jails.

By the mid 1980s, the MM was thought to have around six hundred members and La Nuestra Familia as many as eight hundred.

Like the MM, La Nuestra Familia started to operate on the outside when its members were released. And like them, they based their code on the Cosa Nostra's code of honour.

On the inside looking out: inmates of Texas Dept. of Corrections Prison.

Its members have to swear an oath that puts the gang's interests above all others, and agree that once in there is no way out. Ordinary members are *soldados* who can work their way up the ranks to lieutenant and on to captain, depending on the number of hits achieved. Supreme power is held by 'The General'.

In its war against the MM, La Nuestra Familia allied itself to Black Guerrilla, a gang that had been founded in San Quentin as the Vanguards by George Jackson, a leading member of the Black Panthers.

Not to be outdone, the MM allied itself with Aryan Brotherhood, founded as the Diamond Tooth Gang. As its name suggests it is a white, neo-Nazi gang, which draws its members from imprisoned Hell's Angels and other bike gangs. It is one of the most violent of prison gangs and into protection, extortion and contract killings, both inside and outside prisons.

Also loosely allied to the Aryan Brotherhood is the Texas Syndicate, which was founded by Texan prisoners as a means of self-preservation in 1974. When the original members were released, they returned to Texas where many of them quickly re-offended. They were sent to jail in their home state and quickly became the dominant (and most violent) prison gang in Texas.

In 1985, a fifth major prison gang arrived on the scene – the Consolidated Crip Organization (CCO) – which commanded loyalty from up to fifty thousand men languishing in US prisons all over the country. It wasn't long before their great rivals, the Bloods, established a presence – the United Blood Nation or 'Red Rags', in penitentiaries coast to coast.

Faced with an increasing number of prison murders, the authorities did what they could to clamp down on the gangs and by the middle of the 1990s they were confident enough to hope that prison gangs were a thing of the past.

They were wrong. Prison gangs still flourish. And as long as society sends those who break its laws to jail, they always will. A new prisoner who doesn't join a gang in an American jail won't survive for long.

GANGLAND INTERNATIONAL

THERE are more than one hundred and fifty countries in the United Nations. It is probably a safe bet that in every one of them organized crime is, if not flourishing, then responsible for at least part of the crime rate. From rural Ireland where the IRA, which operates for political ends rather than financial gain, is still a force to be reckoned with, to urban Denmark, where, in 2001, the leader of the Bandidos gang was shot down outside his house: from Taiwan where Triad gangs control most of the organized crime, to South Africa where the trade in illicit diamond buying attracts gangland attention. Everywhere there are gangs.

In some countries they people the shadowy underworld that is their traditional environment: in some they operate with the unofficial connivance of the state. (Many of the men who rubbed shoulders with Boris Yeltsin in post-communist Russia are believed to have had Mafya connections.) In one country, Zimbabwe, they have the official backing of the president. There, gangs of 'War Veterans' are officially empowered by President Mugabe to drive white farmers off the land they have for decades worked so successfully that Zimbabwe supplied grain to much of Central Africa. War Veterans, very few of whom have seen service in any war, and their families have then moved in and returned to the subsistence farming of previous generations. The result has seen the country's once-thriving economy in freefall towards bankruptcy. Such state-sponsored organized crime has a much more devastating effect on a country than old-fashioned gangsters ever could.

This crook's tour of organized crime around the world is the merest tip of the iceberg. Like the one that saw the *Titanic* sink to the ocean floor, what we see can only hint at what lies beneath the surface.

AUSTRALIA

As in Britain, the Prohibition laws that fuelled the gangland disputes in the United States had little effect in Australia. Indeed, for a country whose original settlers were mainly convicted criminals, transported there for their misdemeanours in

Britain, there was surprisingly little organized crime in the country until the Australian government instituted its post-war mass immigration programme. Then, in the 1950s and early 1960s, millions of Europeans were encouraged to leave their homelands and sail to Australia (and New Zealand), their fares hugely subsidized by the governments. Many of the new Australians were British, but thousands of southern Europeans also sailed east, and a few of them took their gangland heritage with them.

That is not to say that there was no gangland activity before that: there was. In the 1920s, for example, Sydney was the theatre of activity of several youth street gangs who ran their own territories. The Surrey Hill Mob, for example, controlled the area that stretched from Surrey Hill to Darlinghurst, and the area around the city's Newtown railway station was the territory of the eponymous Newtown Mob. Members of this gang were employed by the manager of a local theatre to keep unruly patrons in order. It was a logical step for them to move into the protection racket. After all, if they were paid by the manager of one theatre to guard his premises, why should others not pay for the same service?

One of the Newtown Mob's rival gangs, the Railway Gang, operated in the part of central Sydney that ran from Grace Brothers Department Store on Broadway to the Town Hall. The gang's speciality was shoplifting. While some of them distracted the shop assistants with their unruly behaviour, others threw anything

The famous Grace Brothers Department Store, Sydney, target of the shoplifting Railway Gang. (WILLIAM WEST/AFP/Getty Images)

they could get their hands on from the first floor windows to waiting friends below.

Other Australian cities, too, had their gangs and gangsters. In Melbourne, for instance, Joseph Taylor, who rejoiced in the nickname 'Squizzy', worked his way up from petty theft and small time blackmail (an illegal abortionist was one of his first victims) in the early years of the 1900s to be king of the Melbourne underworld in the 1920s. Grog-shop protection and other rackets were the rungs he used on the ladder to the top.

Brothels were also scenes of gangland activity: the 1929 'War of the Brothel Queens' was an incident that would set the scenario for the film of the same name. And, of course, dealing in illicit drugs was something that attracted gangland interest. High quality cocaine, morphine and opium were brought into Queensland from Asia: poorer opium, usually Dutch in origin, was brought in via the western ports of Freemantle and Rottnest from Java.

In Sydney, in the 1920s, much of the street trade in narcotics was under the control of 'Jewey' Freeman, the self-styled King of the Sydney Dope Traffickers. He got some of his supplies from doctors and dentists, often going to their surgeries to do business with his children in tow. He packaged what he bought into small bags which he sold for five shillings, mainly to prostitutes and their clients.

But organized crime did not really become big scale in Australia until transoceanic shipping made the country the hub for the transportation of drugs and other illegal commodities. (By this time, many of the docks in which the liners anchored were under control of coteries who operated inside the dockers' unions, such as Melbourne's Dockies. The little groups blackmailed owners to avoid strike action and ran lists of fictitious workers. From there it was but a small step to theft and armed robbery, extortion and protection rackets.)

The drug trade in Australia

In the early 1960s what trade in drugs there was in New South Wales, the most populous and prosperous of Australia's six states was run by the Calabrian 'Honoured Society' – a gang with its roots in Italy. But in the middle years of the decade, the Italian gang was swamped by an international multi-million crime network that was largely under the control of a partnership forged between big-time Australian gangsters and their contacts in the US Mafia.

Immigration officials may have suspected (indeed known) that several of the American 'businessmen' who walked down the gangplanks of trans-Pacific liners and down the steps of airplanes at international airports were US Mafia men, but they didn't bar them from entering the country. And the Australian police no doubt knew that many of the men the visitors contacted were leading figures in Australian organized crime. But it was not until 1973 when a report by

Mr Justice Moffitt identified organized crime in Australia that most Australians knew that it existed there. By this time it was too late. The connections had been made. The links had been forged. And the US Mafia had launched native-born Australian gangsters on new and lucrative careers.

It was with Mafia backing that Australian gangsters such as Bob Trimbole, Stan 'The Man' Smith and Lennie 'Mr Big' McPherson began to make their fortunes in traditional Mafia activities – international drug trafficking, gambling, extortion and money laundering. They also got into fraud in a big way, and shoplifting on a massive scale, using riffraff from the streets to prey on the cities' big department stores, paying them a fraction of what they stole was actually worth. They then sold on what they bought at hugely marked-up prices via small time crooks, in grog-shops, markets and other outlets where there is no way of tracing the provenance of what's on offer. And when they realized there was money to be made in the trade in rare animals, the new-style gangs were quickly into it.

A partnership is begun

One of the Mafia men who came in from the United States was Chicago gangster Joe Testa. In fact, he was one of the first to establish a partnership between the US Mafia and the Australian underworld. He flew into Sydney in 1965, his visit laying the foundations for what was to come. In 1968, Smith and another Australian mobster George Freeman returned the visit. After being lavishly entertained in Chicago, they were flown to Las Vegas for an extravagant freebie paid for by Testa and his mob.

The party that Lennie McPherson threw for Testa on a return visit to Australian, at Watson's Bay's Fisherman's Bay, was just as lavish. And the finale there was a fitting tribute from the Australians to the guest of honour. In true gangster fashion, Testa was presented with a huge cake, with the words 'Welcome Joe' iced across the top. Had it been a Hollywood movie, then a few moments later, a machine-gun-toting figure would have burst from the cake. But it wasn't the sound of gunfire that rang round the room, it was the words of 'For he's a jolly good fellow!'

Shortly after the party, Lennie McPherson, the 'Mr Big' of his nickname, crossed the Pacific to cement the relationship. It was drugs, of course, that were at the heart of the relationship. But there was a cog in the wheels of the relationship between the Americans and the Australians. The Australians were proving slow to give up their independence.

Joe Testa, himself, was on the payroll of another, more powerful US gangster, Jimmy Fratianno (known as 'The Weasel' because of his thin features and later to turn informer).

In 1967, Fratianno had sent one of his lieutenants, George 'Duke' Countis to take up permanent residence in Australia. Among the first men Countis contacted when he got there was an Australian drug smuggler, Murray Riles. Not long afterwards a deal was negotiated with the heroin suppliers in the Golden Triangle, the area of Thailand, Laos and Burma where much of the opium poppies that are used to manufacture illegal heroin are grown.

Once the contacts with the growers had been established, the pair set up an extensive smuggling system to bring the drugs in from Thailand to New South Wales. The smugglers relied on ships, secret airstrips and occasionally couriers to get the drugs into the country. (The use of couriers was seen as a last resort. Being caught smuggling drugs in several Asian countries carries at worst the death sentence or at best a lengthy jail sentence, usually in a cell that in the words of someone who was caught, 'made the urinal in a Thailand brothel seem like the Hilton by comparison'.)

When the infrastructure was in place, the US Mafia expected the money to roll in, but the Australians were seen to be slow in tapping into this new source of money. Something had to be done.

In 1971, during one of McPherson's visits to Chicago, Fratianno handed him a suitcase ('A little something to get things moving again.'). The suitcase contained $1 million. Soon heroin was flowing into the country. It made the gangsters rich, but the cost in human life was terrible. Tens of thousands of Australians became addicts, and to feed their habit were forced to turn to petty crime and larceny, with a corresponding rise in the crime rate that horrified the ordinary man in the street.

Heroin is not the only drug that is used by Australians. In the glitzy world of the 1980s and 1990s, cocaine was the drug of choice among affluent users with hundred dollar bills to roll up and stick up their nose. In the less grim housing estates that skirt the cities, crack cocaine is widely used.

The other drug that brings Australian gangsters much of their income is marijuana. It is estimated that between half and one million Australians, mostly under the age of thirty, are regular users (regular being at least once a month). Nowadays, it is widely tolerated by the police: there was a time when smoking it carried a hefty fine or jail sentence.

Making millions

Most of what is smoked is grown locally, especially by Calabrian immigrants who live in Griffith, a small New South Wales town, three hundred and fifty kilometres north-east of the capital Canberra. Growers there have made millions from supplying the soft drug to users all over the country. One of the problems with having millions of having so much money is getting rid of it without attracting the attention of the authorities. Some of the men built themselves splendid houses in and around the town which are affectionately known as 'grass castles'.

One grower, Bob Trimbole, devised an ingenious scheme to account for his millions. He used his money to bribe jockeys, arrange for horses to be doped and manipulated the odds so that he knew which horse would win which race. Trimbole placed his bets accordingly and when asked by the tax man where his money came from, had all the evidence to 'prove' that it was mostly gambling winnings.

Other Australian rackets

Drugs may account for the most of Australian gangsters' income, but they make big bucks from other scams, too. Among them is wildlife smuggling.

Australia has fauna that is unique. After the landmass that is now the country broke off from one of the two prehistoric continents, millions of years ago, many species evolved that are today found only in Australia.

In the 1970s, Australian gangsters realized that there was big money to be made in exporting koalas, kangaroos, parrots, sulphur-crested cockatoos, snakes and other species, the export of which was strictly controlled by the government.

It wasn't long before the ships and planes that had brought illegal drugs into the country and had gone home with empty holds, were sailing or flying off with these and other exotic creatures aboard. The trade continues to this day and is handled with the same efficiency as the heroin smuggling is. Sometimes, no money changes hands – the birds and animals being traded for heroin.

Some of these creatures, the galah, for instance, are regarded as pests in their native land and can be captured free. Rare parrots and sulphur-crested cockatoos cost a few dollars at most. But collectors in Asia and the United States are willing to pay hundreds, sometimes thousands of dollars, for them. One American importer, Vinnie Teresa, reckoned that he could have sold the birds he paid £3,000 in Australia for around $2 million in the States had the cargo not been seized by Customs officials.

In 1984, Teresa agreed to turn informer rather than stand trial for conspiring to smuggle rare birds into the US. The information he gave led to US officials smashing an Australian smuggling ring called 'The Swiss Connection', intercepting a consignment of around one hundred and fifty snakes, lizards and crocodiles.

That was twenty years ago. Despite that and other successes, the wildlife smuggling gangs still continue to make millions of dollars a year from the trade.

'Kangaroo Gangs'

Another activity that is more or less unique to Australian gangs is shoplifting, which in most countries is considered a trivial offence that might merit a small fine, apart from for the most serious and persistent offenders who may find themselves in jail – for a few weeks at most.

But when it is practised on a huge and well-organized scale, shoplifting can yield millions. In London, 'Kangaroo Gangs' – teams of Australian-trained shoplifters – are so effective that Scotland Yard has a special team dedicated to weeding them out.

The mastermind behind many of the gangs is known as 'The Duke' in

Sydney where he had his base. His men would recruit likely-looking candidates from the less salubrious bars and clubs and train them in various shoplifting techniques. Some couples are taught how to fool jewellers that they have just got engaged and are looking for an engagement or wedding rings. They are shown how to create a slight diversion and take advantage of it to run out of the shop with a tray of the best of what was on offer. Another jeweller's shop scam is to Blu-Tack a small but valuable piece of jewellery under a suitable ridge to be collected later by a seemingly unconnected partner in crime.

Dress shops are also a source of considerable income to the Kangaroo Gangs. Assuming that several can be stolen from the same shop, the same dresses can be returned to the same shop over the course of the next few days and a cash refund demanded.

Individually each theft doesn't yield a great deal. But as they say in Scotland, 'Many a mickle maks a muckle' and the Kangaroo Gangs' various scams mount up, making 'The Duke' a millionaire several times over and providing a very good living for individual gang members.

A con artist par excellence

No section, no matter how brief, on organized crime in Australia would be complete without a mention of Ivan Markovic, an East European immigrant to Australia who ingratiated himself into the upper echelons of the gangster world in Australia and the United States.

After a few years in Australia where he operated on the fringes of the gangsters' world. Markovic realized that many wealthy people had two fatal flaws: vanity and a desire for recognition.

He opened an office in New York, close to the United Nations' building, in the guise of The Knights of Malta, which is, in fact, a respected and legitimate papal order that dates back centuries to the Crusades.

That done, he approached several wealthy Australians, requesting donations for the organization: not the real Knights, but the bogus ones of his imagination. He was so convincing about the good works the Order was responsible for, that many of the men he approached got out their cheque books and obliged. The money went straight into Markovic's pocket.

In exchange, his victims, business-men and lawyers among them, were initiated as full 'Knights of Malta'. They were given opulent regalia, diplomatic passports and assured that as members of the noble papal order they had diplomatic immunity. Markovic even flew a group of initiates to Rome where they stayed in one of the city's best hotels before being bussed, in their robes, to the initiation ceremony which was con-ducted by a 'Cardinal of the Order' at the Basilica di St Nicola. They flew home, their wallets considerably lighter, blissfully unaware that the 'cardinal' was a conman of Mark-ovic's acquaintance and the 'Basilica di St Nicola' an abandoned casino that had been hired for the night and suitably decorated. (As Markovic said, 'It's amazing what you can get away with in candlelight!')

Things started to unravel in Australia when one of the 'Knights', Bela Csidei, one of the Griffith marijuana growers, was arrested, and tried to escape prosecution by claiming diplomatic immunity as a Knight of Malta. He was eventually jailed, but it was through him that Markovic began to operate his scam in the United States.

One of Csidei's US contacts was Rudi Tham, the leader of the San Francisco Teamsters Union, which had widespread Mafia connections. Tham put his hand deep into the Teamsters' funds to pay for a knighthood and was only too happy to oblige when Markovic asked him to spread the word about the Order, the good works it did and to hint that generous donations to the Order's charities would be suitably rewarded.

Most of the wealthy men Tham knew were top-of-the-tree US gangsters, among them Jimmy Fratianno, the man who gave Lennie McPherson $1 million in a suitcase to oil the wheels of the Mafia-Australia heroin-smuggling deal. Fratianno was no fool. He knew a scam when he saw one. Rudi Tham tried to convince him that Markovic's Knights of Malta was on the level. 'It's a very exclusive order. I just got in myself,' Tham is reputed to have said to try to convince the Mafia man. To which Fratianno replied, 'Bullshit. Not if you're in it. Sounds like a high-class scam.'

But rather than give Markovic away, Fratianno decided to use him for schemes of his own, one of which is said to have brought Frank Sinatra into contact with the US Mafia, in an episode that was to haunt him for the rest of his life.

Markovic continued his scam until he was exposed for the fraudster he was, in 1985. He fled to Europe and lived the rest of his life in obscurity. Few if any of the men he parted from their money in exchange for a 'knighthood' ever asked to see how it was being used.

If Markovic's career proves anything, it is that even the most hardened of criminals crave society's approval.

On the Streets

As in every major country in the world, Australia has its street gangs, but with a population of just fifty million in a country that covers an area of over seven and a half million square kilometres they are less of a problem than, say, in California which has a population density nine times greater.

The gun culture that has infected gangland in other countries and has seen a corresponding increase in the use of firearms in turf wars is not so prevalent in Australia, although police statistics suggest it is increasing.

Street gangs in Sydney, Melbourne and the other major cities are involved in muggings, mobile phone theft, theft from cars and other low-level crimes: and, more seriously, drug distribution and dealing.

The gangs are attractive to underachieving school children and the young disaffected unemployed. By the time they are in their mid-twenties, most members have left, either getting themselves onto some sort of job ladder, or (especially in Sydney) have drifted into a life of petty crime, willing members of street gangs in the city being used as foot soldiers for organized crime syndicates.

As in other parts of the world, street gangs in Australia tend to be neighbourhood and hence ethnic in origin. They share the same mores that are found their counterparts on the streets of London and New York – body marking, sign language and styles of dressing – the globalization of television and pop culture has seen to that.

CANADA

When Italians started to emigrate to North America in vast numbers at the end of the nineteenth century and the start of the twentieth, not all of them went to the United States. Many of them settled in Canada, and just as those who settled in the States brought their Mafia mentality with them, so did their cousins who settled north of the border.

They got involved in the usual Mafia businesses – extortion, corruption, prostitution, illegal gambling, protection and the like, but when Prohibition was introduced into the United States in January 1920, brewing and liquor production and consumption remained legal in Canada. If the US mobsters couldn't turn out enough illicit booze of its own to satisfy the insatiable demand, Canadian distillers and brewers were only too happy to step in and fill the gap.

The only problem was that exporting liquor into the United States was a direct violation of the Volstead Act that had ushered in Prohibition. In reality, though, smuggling liquor into the US was a comparatively risk-free business. By the 1920s, the automobile was in widespread use, and it proved to be the perfect means of transport for bootlegging because of its size and mobility. And as the border between the two countries runs for thousands of miles and is unfenced, it was and is impossible to patrol efficiently. What chance there was of getting caught was overshadowed by the huge profits there were to be made. Cheaply produced tax-free Canadian whisky and other liquors sold for outrageous sums in the United States.

It is impossible to imagine that Canadian gangsters were not going to get involved. One of the first to see the opportunity for bootlegging (the word derives from the practice of hiding a bottle of alcohol in the leg of a boot) was Rocco Perri who started one of Canada's biggest and most efficient booze-smuggling operations. He became so good at getting huge quantities into the States that he was known as 'the king of the bootleggers' and 'Canada's Al Capone'. It was Perri who, more than any other gangster, put Canada on the international organized-crime map.

Like Capone, Perri got his start in 'Little Italy' – not New York's Little Italy, but the area in Hamilton, Ontario where Italian immigrants lived. He broke his criminal teeth in the Black Hand extortion racket, but unlike ninety-nine per cent of his fellow gangsters, eventually decided that violence was bad for business. This belief was instilled in him when there was a spate of bombings in Hamilton's Little Italy that left entire families crushed to death in the ruins of their apartments. Perri was so moved by the incident he that he swore to use 'elegant persuasion' rather than physical force to get his way.

During Prohibition, he had to struggle to keep his organization independent of US Mafia control, but he managed to amass a fortune which he invested in true Mafia fashion in gambling and running protection rackets. When Prohibition came to an end in 1933, the US Mafia bosses were no longer dependent on their Canadian counterparts, but even so, they were still determined to extend their control of criminal activities across the border. But despite their best efforts, Perri managed to keep Hamilton firmly in his grasp.

'The Egg'

After his death, the US Mafia intensified their efforts to extend its influence into Canada. One link that they established was between New York's Bonanno family and Canadian mobster Vincenzo 'The Egg' Cotroni. (He acquired that sobriquet when he lost his hair! It was not a moniker he relished and woe betide anyone who used it in his presence. He preferred to be called 'Vic'.)

Cotroni was born in Italy and came to Canada with his parents in 1924. His father, Nicodemo, needing to support his family, soon got involved in bootlegging, and Vincenzo eventually followed him into a life of crime. With each arrest for a variety of minor offences, Vic and his brothers Frank and Pep settled deeper and deeper into their criminal careers.

The 1930s saw him move to Montreal where he and his family had invested the proceeds of their bootlegging and other activities in the nightclub business. He was soon into loan sharking, prostitution, gambling and extortion. Later, he moved into the food distribution business which helped him tighten his control of the city.

He was held in such respect in Montreal's underworld that he earned the nickname 'Le Perrain' ('The Godfather'). The city was a hive of gangland activity. Not all the gangs were Italian in origin. Some were French and others had their roots in Britain. Whenever the inevitable tensions threatened to spill into violence, 'The Egg' used his considerable charm and negotiating skills to keep the peace, while at the same time seizing every opportunity to maximize his own profits.

Obviously a man of such criminal and diplomatic skills came to the notice of the Mafia in the United States, and in 1953, don Joe Bonanno decided that it was time that the two of them did business. He sent his driver and close associate, Carmine Galante, to meet with the Canadian in a Montreal pizzeria and put a proposition to him – a proposition that Cotroni could not refuse.

Until that time, the Canadian

Mafia don Joe Bonnano, aka Joey Bananas.

gangster had only dabbled in drugs smuggling. Galante suggested it was time for him to move into it in a much bigger way: he suggested that Montreal could become the centre of the Mafia's drug trafficking. The US authorities were beginning to clamp down on the traditional routes of bringing drugs into the States. Recalling the good old days of Prohibition when it has been as easy as pie to smuggle liquor over the border, Joe Bonanno had realized that Montreal would be the ideal take-off point for bringing heroin into the United States.

Cotroni agreed to be involved. But he also had to accept that Galante, acting for Joe Bonanno, was to be the boss of the operation. He (Galante) opened an electronics store in the city as a front for the operation. But his tenure didn't last long. Within two years, a new crime-fighting mayor, Jean Drapeaux, was elected to office in Montreal. He had Galante deported to the States on the grounds that he could not explain exactly what his occupation was: as one of he policemen involved in the deportation is reported to have said, 'He could have written down all he knew about the electronics business on the back of a two-cent stamp and still had room for a Hail Mary or two and a couple of Mea Culpas.'

The next man sent by Bonanno to front the operation was soon sent packing. And so, in 1957, he turned to Vic Cotroni, who could never be deported from his native land, and asked him to run the operation directly. 'The Egg' accepted, in exchange for a large share of the profits. But in the dog-eat-dog world that is gangsterland, he had to accept Bonanno and therefore the US Mafia as a major player in the Canadian crime game.

Shortly afterwards, one of the most famous drug smuggling schemes was put into operation, immortalized in the book and film *The French Connection*. Heroin from Turkey was smuggled into Marseilles, from where it was shipped to Montreal and then taken across the border into the US.

Treating everyone equally

Cotroni made millions from the operation. In a gesture to show off his wealth to fellow denizens of the Canadian underworld, and to show the US Mafia that although he owed them, he still considered himself to have a comparatively free hand in Montreal, he built a stunning house in the Ontario countryside. The mansions combined the functions of family home and conference centre for the Canadian criminal fraternity. The chandelier-hung meeting room had a hand-made walnut table with seats for more than two dozen people. And, ever the diplomat, Cotroni had his own master bedroom and all the guest bedrooms built the same size, each one decorated as lavishly as the others. That way, he reasoned, no one ever need feel snubbed by being put in a room that was in any way inferior to the others.

Despite the fact that it was supposedly Joe Bonanno who pulled the strings from New York, Cotroni and his brothers Frank and Pep along with their close friends Paolo Violi

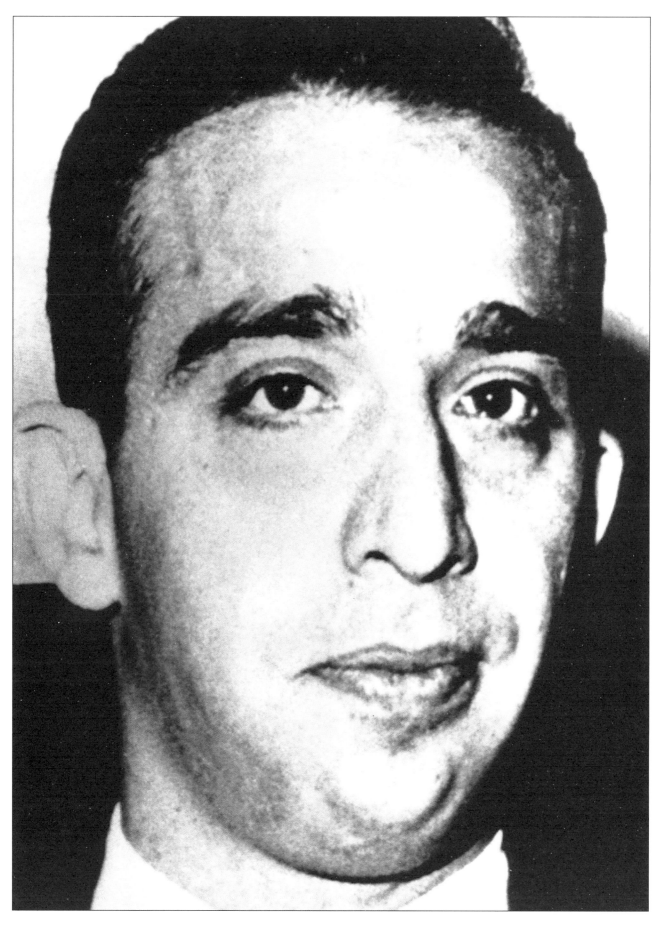

*A young Carmine 'Lilo' Galante, one of the mafia's top godfathers,
at the time facing 39 yrs in jail for extortion and racketeering.*

and his brothers ruled the roost in Montreal, with their close associate Johnny Papalia running things in Hamilton.

The money rolled in, not just from the French Connection but from the other scams they ran. One of them, though, did cause something of a scandal. In 1967, the Canadian government hosted the Expo Exhibition, an event that attracted worldwide publicity. So, too, did the beef that Cotroni, through one of his food-processing companies, supplied to several of the caterers. The men running Expo may have paid for beef: they got horsemeat.

Even before that, things had started to go awry. In the early years of the decade, Pep Cotroni had been sent down for drugs smuggling after he unwittingly employed an undercover FBI agent as a courier. In the United States, Carmine Galante was sentenced to twelve years for drugs-related offences. And then, Joe Bonanno had to go into hiding when his plot to oust the other New York families and establish himself as capo di capi was rumbled.

Bonanno came out of hiding in the late 1960s and made his peace with the other Mafia families, but Cotroni's moment at the top of the Canadian crime tree was coming to an end. He knew that he couldn't go on forever, and had decided to groom Paolo Viola as his successor, unaware that his favourite was the subject of an undercover investigation by the authorities.

Paolo had had no idea that the man he had rented an apartment to, above a pizzeria he owned, was an undercover agent, known as Menard. The gangster and the cop struck up an unlikely friendship after Paolo had been impressed by the way Menard haggled about the rent. The detective took advantage of his relationship to bug Paolo's office, and when he had accumulated enough evidence, he had the gangster arrested. On discovering who was responsible, Paolo Viola's men wanted to take Menard out. Viola put an end to the plan. 'He's a stand up guy,' he is reported as saying. 'He's a better fucking soldier than the rest of you.'

It wasn't just Paolo Viola who Detective Menard nailed. The tapes also implicated 'The Egg' himself in a minor scam that earned him a six-month jail sentence. Sitting alone and brooding in his cell, Cotroni turned his anger towards Viola. His anger intensified later, when both men were out of jail, and Paolo started to talk too much about Cotroni's business affairs.

In January 1978 when Paolo Viola was playing cards, two masked men entered the room. Just before a gun was put against his head one of the men is said to have kissed him on the cheek: a second later the trigger was pulled. Everyone assumed Vic Cotroni was behind the assassination, but when four Sicilians were later convicted of conspiracy, the finger was pointed at Nicholas Rizzuto. Rizzuto had been a friend of 'The Egg' but had started to put together a serious power base that was attracting members of the city's Sicilian community.

Among the lavish floral tributes in the thirty-one limousines that followed the funeral cortege, there was one from Cotroni and another from Carmine Galante, but the most lavish one was from Viola's father. Shaped like a clock with its hands stopped at 7.32, the time when Paulo had been murdered, it was spectacular, even by gangland standards.

Viola Senior was no stranger to gangland killings. In 1977 his youngest son, Francesco, was backed against a wall in one of the family's importation company buildings by two contract killers and was shot in the face. Three years later, the last surviving brother stopped his car at traffic lights in the city. A motorcyclist drew up alongside and shot him in the head. He survived, but three months later when he was sitting at the kitchen table with his sons, he was killed by a single shot to the heart, fired from a vantage point across the road.

Not long after Paulo's funeral, Carmine Galante, who having served his sentence had been released, was gunned down in a classic Mafia

The body of Carmine Galante lies where it has fallen,
gunned down in a Brooklyn restaurant by rival mobsters, 1978.

killing, in a Brooklyn restaurant. Next to vanish from the scene was Frank Cotroni, Vic's brother, who was sentenced to a fifteen-year maximum stretch in prison.

As his hold on Montreal's crime scene began to slip from his grasp, Vic Cotroni was an increasingly lonely and desperate man. By the time the 1980s arrived, he found that there were several upstarts competing for his position as king of the Montreal underworld. In an effort to impress them and re-establish himself as Numero Uno, he decided to try to muscle in on the criminal world in Toronto, where a gangster called Paul Volpe was in charge. In November 1983, Volpe was found dead in the boot of his car in a car park at Pearson International Airport. It was assumed that Cotroni was behind the assassination, but no evidence was ever produced.

Had he been younger, Vic Cotroni would have been able to take advantage of the vacancy at the top, but he was now an elderly man, and most of his former associates were either behind bars or had long since retired. He died a year after Paul Volpe's murder, his Montreal empire crumbling around him. He had made a fortune from his life in crime. In one account alone, used for laundering drug money, there was more than $80 million!

His brother Frank, tried to drive his family name back into the pole position in Montreal's gangland, but by this time gangs from the Middle East and China had gained more than a foothold on the crime ladder. As they climbed it, the Cotroni name declined and has now been more or less consigned to the history books.

Canadian gangland today

Today, gangland crime is common all over Canada: indeed the country has become something of a Mecca for fugitive criminals. A recent report suggests that it has become a refuge for Asian Mob men and the Chinese Mafia. One of them, Lai Changxing, arrived in the country in 1999 bringing with him the proceeds from his criminal empire in the Fujian province in China.

In Toronto, the Mafia, which was more or less unchallenged for decades, now has to compete with the Russian Mafya, Jamaican Posses, bike gangs, Vietnamese mobsters and Colombians selling cocaine by the kilo.

In Montreal, the internecine bike gang wars saw violence spill onto the street, until the Angels led by Maurice Boucher emerged victorious. But Boucher was sentenced to at least twenty-five years in prison in 2000, leaving a vacuum at the top of the organization. The Angels' main rivals for power in the city is the Mafia family run by Vito Rizzuto, who had taken over from Frank Cotroni and who is said to have established an alliance with the powerful Siderno group in Toronto. In a case that echoes down the decade to the world of Al Capone, Rizzuto was charged with tax evasion, but a week before the trial was due to open, he reached an out-of-court settlement with Revenue Canada.

Across the country, in Vancouver, Asian gangs compete for control of the lucrative cocaine market, with all the usual hallmarks of the game. One of the most spectacular of these occurred on 20 December, 1998 – the Sunday before Christmas. As Bhupinder Johal, one of the leading players in the cocaine game, was dancing in the city's Palladium nightclub a gunman walked behind him and shot him behind the left ear. Despite the fact that there were three hundred people in the club, that there were CCTV cameras trained on all the exits, and the murder weapon, a semi-automatic pistol, was found abandoned on a bar stool, no one was ever charged with the murder.

Johal and his gang, the Diablos, had been competing with the Dosanjh Brothers for control of the cocaine market in the city for years. The competition was marked with the usual gangland killings, which at least one tragic consequence. A few years before Bhupinder's killing, his neighbour had been shot twenty-nine times while out walking his dog. The Dosanjh gunman responsible, who later died of a heroin overdose, had mistaken the innocent man for the Asian drug dealer.

THE COLOMBIAN CONNECTION

No book of gang, gangsters and gangland would be complete without a mention of the Colombian Connection, as drugs are a major, if not *the* major, source of revenue for many of the world's gangs. It was drugs that brought the Italian Mafia into contact with the Asian gangs. It was through drugs that the Cosa Nostra in the United States moved northwards into Canada.

The three main centres of drug production are the Golden Triangle of Southeast Asia, the Golden Crescent in Afghanistan and Pakistan, both of which supply heroin, and the drug fields of South America that supply addicts the world over with most of the cocaine they use. (There are also areas of Africa that produce both these drugs, but on a much reduced scale.)

It has been pointed out that the men who control drug production in Colombia, the South American country that shares borders with Panama, Venezuela, Brazil, Peru and Ecuador, have blurred any distinction there is between gangsters and terrorists. For decades, drug production in the country and in the rest of Latin America was little more than a cottage industry, supplying local demand and exporting some north, through Central America into the United States. But by some time in the 1960s, the foundation stones had been put in place that were to turn that cottage industry into a multi-billion industry run by some of the most ruthless men in the world. Cocaine produced in Latin America is sold on street corners in every town and city in the world. It is an industry that employs hundreds of thousands of people and has an annual income that is equal to the gross national product of several developing countries – combined.

Many of the people are 'mules' – the men and women who carry the cocaine into market countries. Sometimes it is cunningly concealed in suitcases and baggage. But increasingly sophisticated technology makes this increasingly easy to detect. Colombian cocaine is often carried inside the mule's body – packed in contraceptives and swallowed, washed down with copious amounts of water. It is extraordinary just how much cocaine can be stored for a short time in the human digestive system. One person can bring in drugs with a street value of several hundred thousands of dollars in this way. While it is safer than smuggling it in bags and baggage it is still risky. Should one of the packs burst before it has been excreted, the mule experiences a massive drug overdose, usually with fatal results. And just as sophisticated technology (and well-trained sniffer dogs) make traditional methods easier to detect, so have the mules become easier to track. When a suspect is stopped it is a simple matter for Customs men to detain them until nature takes its course and the evidence is produced. (In some difficult cases, a strong enema does the trick.) The penalties are for drug smuggling are harsh (it carries the death sentence in some countries), but the rewards are so high, that there is no shortage of recruits.

The drugs barons

By the late 1970s, the drugs barons were in business. There are extremely well organized. They have to be: the expansion of the drug production industry from raw material (the Southeast Asia plant) to coca paste and then to cocaine base before being transformed into cocaine proper (cocaine hydrochloride) is one that needs careful monitoring. The men behind the huge increase in cocaine production on Colombia planned the expansion carefully and it paid: the earning potential was vast.

Originally operating independently of each other, the drug barons forged a cartel in 1981 after members of the many terrorist groups that plague the country kidnapped the sister of one of them. The group, M-19, was named after the election of 19 April 1970, which they claimed, had been rigged. They quasi-military men snatched Marta Ochoa Vasquez, the sister of Jorge Ochoa, one of the most powerful of all Colombian drugs barons. They also tried, but failed, to kidnap Carlos Lehrer Rivas, perhaps the best narcotics smuggler in the game. M-19 demanded $1 million for Vasquez's release.

The drugs barons met in Cali, a town one hundred and twenty or so kilometres inland from the coast, to discuss the situation. The men agreed to work together to fight M-19. They had a leaflet printed and distributed widely among the population stating that they were forming what they called a 'mafia' to fight the terrorists and that they intended to create an army of two thousand trained killers to take the fight to M-19. The drugs barons' men swept into operation, brutally terrorizing anyone the suspected of being either a member or a supporter of the organization. Within a few weeks, M-19 gave up and Marta Vasquez was released.

Colombian police pile up captured cocaine ready to burn.

Their raison d'etre satisfied, the barons could have disbanded, but they had realized the advantages to be had from cooperating with each other, and the temporary union became a permanent cartel.

For the rest of the decade, two individual men and one powerful family dominated the cartel. Pablo Escobar was in charge of security and managing the production of the finished cocaine. Gonzalo Rodriguez oversaw the importation of cocoa paste from suppliers across the borders with Bolivia and Peru. And the Ochoa family was responsible for smuggling the finished cocaine out of the country. Between them, *los duenos del cupo* (holders of the quota) controlled a drug production business that was second only to the Golden Triangle in the money it produced.

Medellin, around three hundred kilometres from the border with Panama, was chosen as the centre, and from there a vast amount of high-grade cocaine and the more addictive crack cocaine was shipped by various means to all over the world. The group became so powerful that when the Colombian government tried to take measures to control the cartel, the cartel effectively declared war on the government, arranging for the deaths of members of parliament and the judiciary at will. When Colombia's Supreme Court was debating an extradition treaty with the United States, Escobar sent in M-19 with which he had made peace and to whom he is said to have paid $5 million to implement the reign of terror he instituted. The Colombian

president sent in troops in to end the siege. But by the time they arrived, more M-19 guns had killed sixty hostages. In the end, most of the M-19 men were themselves killed by government guns.

The M-19 is not the only terrorist organization the cartel paid for services rendered. Money earned from the cocaine industry has gone to pay members of the communist Revolutionary Armed Forces of Colombia to guard the cartel's Tranquilandia – the production camps it operates on an island in Yari, a river that flows through dense rainforest before eventually entering a tributary of the mighty Amazon.

Escobar was like a feudal king, In Peru alone, more that three hundred thousand men and women were on his payroll, tending the coca crops. Inside Columbia, his private army of terrorist guerrillas was backed by his own troops who between them could muster more than enough firepower to challenge the government. Anyone who dared to challenge the cartel became a target for its guns. When one Medellin judge, Carlos Jiminez, dared to suggest that judicial corruption had led to the early release from prison of a member of the Ochoa family, he was found, handcuffed, blindfold and gagged – and shot in the head ten times.

When the cartel was suspected of being behind the assassination of a newly installed justice minister, the backlash was such that the cartel's bosses arranged a 'business trip' to Panama. From there they flew all over the world, establishing links with police chiefs in Peru, Honduras,

A young Pablo Escobar, boss of the Medellin cocaine cartel, accompanied by bodyguard.

Cuba, Haiti, Brazil and Bolivia. At the same time, a splinter syndicate, the Cali, based in the town of that name, five hundred kilometres south of Medellin, began to build up a distribution network into Europe through Spain and Portugal.

Meanwhile, back in Colombia, government troops, working alongside men from the US Drug Enforcement Agency tried to go deep into the rainforest to track down and eliminate the cartel's men, but they were usually beaten back. Even if they were successful and a refining and processing centre was destroyed, the cartel simply moved on and set up new centres in other parts of the jungle.

The Cali Cartel

In the early 1980s, the US cocaine market had been divided up between the Medellin cartel who controlled distribution on Florida and the Cali gang who ran things in New York. But in the mid-1980s, with the US market approaching saturation point, a fight for supremacy broke out between the two that was to last for the rest of the decade and into the 1990s.

In 1993, Pablo Escobar was killed by Cali gangsters. Other members of the Medellin cartel were either in jail (as a result of Cali tip-offs) or had shared the same fate as Escobar. Cali has now taken over from Medellin as the centre of Colombian cocaine production, at first under the control of the two Orejuela brothers, since 1995 (when one of them was jailed) directly commanded by Miguel Orejuela.

The Cali has established a presence in every major industrial nation in the world. In the US they use Jamaican Posse gangs such as New York's Shower Posse and, in the UK, Yardie gangs are known to be on the Cali's payroll.

US sources believe that Posse gangs are responsible for over a thousand murders a year, many of them committed in inter-gang wars with one Posse mob trying to muscle in on another's patch. Murder, it seems, is simply seen as part of the job!

NEW ZEALAND

A famous British actress once remarked that when she landed in New Zealand, it was early closing day. Somehow the remark struck a chord and helped to lodge in the world's collective imagination a picture of New Zealand as an oh-so-quiet country where nothing ever happens.

Travel posters show New Zealand as a beautiful country of snow-covered peaks reflected in ripple-free mirror lakes, of hot springs and cool cities, of deserted beaches and sun-dappled seas. But anyone who has ever read *Once Were Warriors* and similar books by New Zealand authors will know that beyond Auckland's glittering harbour lie some of the bleakest housing estates in the world. There and in similar estates in the country's cities, thousands of people live hopeless and bitter lives.

New Zealand has always had its criminal underworld run by gangs and gangsters just like in every country of the world. The first were

State housing block in South Auckland. ©FOTOPRESS/Dean Purcel

probably the Irish gangs, who fought for control of the docks before World War Two. The Mafia operates in New Zealand, of course, and Asian gangs have a presence there along with Hells Angels, who have two chapters, one in Auckland and another in Wanganui, and other biker gangs who tend to affiliate themselves with the Angels or their main rivals, the Highway 61 Gang. In addition, there are several local gangs such as the Mongerel Mob, Black Power and the King Cobras, all of which recruit their members from among discontented Maoris.

A recent phenomenon

According to Greg Newbold, senior lecturer in Sociology at Canterbury University, it is only in comparatively recent times that organized crime became a specific problem in New Zealand. The first sign of it came with the Mr Asia gang that operated a drug distribution network in Australasia during the 1970s. Although it was smashed with the arrest of its leading members in the United Kingdom in 1979, organized crime continued to grow.

A number of smaller gangs had operated in the shadows of Mr Asia and by the 1980s various motorcycle and street gangs had moved in to fill the gap left by Mr Asia's demise. As the 1980s proceeded they moved to feed the demand for the newer drugs that came onto the market – marijuana, LSD and methamphetamine. Today these and other drugs are the main source of the gangs' incomes which are supplemented by money made from night clubs, massage parlours, the supply of firearms and services such as debt collecting, intimidating those who are unwilling or unable to pay to find the money somehow.

The oldest gang in the country is now the Hells Angels. The Auckland Hells Angels Motorcycle Club was the first to be formed outside the United States, in 1961. Two of America's other bike gangs, the Outlaws and the Bandidos, are also present in New Zealand. While it is not the parent organizations that are involved in organized crime, there is little doubt that members of the individual chapters are responsible much of the crime in the country.

The second major locus of organized crime there is within the Asian community. It is here where the most significant growth has been witnessed as a result of major influxes of people of Asian extraction in recent years. The population of ethnic Chinese in New Zealand more than doubled between 1981 and 2001, and today around a third of all residency approvals are to people from North Asia.

The majority of them are law-abiding peaceful people, but where there are Chinese immigrants there are Triad gangs. Among the Hong Kong Chinese who emigrated to New Zealand as far back as the early 1970s were members of the 14K Triad gang. They have been joined by other triad families such as the San Yee On and the Wo. These and other criminal gangs from Thailand, Vietnam, Malaysia, Singapore and Japan are all involved in intimidation, extortion,

money laundering, gambling, fraud, burglary, receiving, prostitution, robbery, gun smuggling and immigration offences

Almost all the significant heroin seizures since the late 1980s have involved Asians from one or other of the gangs, and in the 1990s there was an eight-fold increase in the number of Asians arrested by the police. Today, on a per capita basis, Asians have the second-highest police apprehension rate in the country, behind the Maori.

The Maori gangs

There is increasing concern in the country at the apparent collusion between the Asian gangs and local ones such as the Mongrel Mob. In one worrying case the police found out that one Asian gang, 14K, was trying to use members of the Monger Mob to fulfil contracts on two police officers.

The Mongrel Mob is probably the most widespread of the Maori gangs, its tentacles stretching throughout the country. Not far behind are the Black Power Gang and the Nomads. The fourth major NZ gang, the King Cobra, is active around the Auckland area. Its members consider themselves 'quiet rebels'. As one member said, 'We hate the government but we prefer to say so rather than commit crimes.'

Joining one or other of the Maori gangs is not a matter of turning up and applying for membership. The chapters of some of them demand that would-be recruits submit themselves to a ritual beating, which goes on until he faints in pain or pleads for the punches to stop. If he faints, he's in. If he pleads for mercy, he is sent packing. Some King Cobras force recruits to have their faces decorated with tattoos, a process that is extremely painful. A few gangs force all their members to pool their welfare payments to fund the purchase of weapons and drugs.

The native gangs feed on Maori discontent, instilling in their members a belief that 'the white man' has let them down and inculcating in them a disregard for society's mores. When the gangs first came to public note, many New Zealanders saw them as a symptom of their own failure to involve them in society and there was a tendency to look on them as high-spirited, deprived kids.

This perception started to change when it was pointed out that between 1993 and 1997, there were twenty-three gang slayings in New Zealand and that the Maori gangs control the cultivation and distribution of cannabis, which gave them a multi-million dollar income every year.

Rivalry between the gangs is intense, especially between the Black Power Gang and the Mongrel Mob. As far back as the 1970s Black Power members invaded a pub where the Mongrel Mob used to hang out, just outside Auckland. The ensuing battle saw axes, chains, cut-throat razors and metal baseball bats being put to lethal use. In another outburst of violence a few months later, guns

Police officer searches the car of two members of the Mongrel Mob near Wairoa. The gang members were in town for a Tangi (funeral) for a Mongrel Mob member who died after a gang confrontation in the town.
©*FOTOPRESS/David James*

were fired. Explosives were used with tragic effect when a gang of Mongrels bombed a van that they thought was occupied by Black Power members. In the event, it wasn't and an innocent man was killed.

The New Zealand police are determined to do what they can to bring the gangs to heel. In one co-ordinated raid to try to get to grips with the illegal trade in methamphetamine, hundreds of officers swooped on seventy-eight addresses on both North and South Islands. In another raid over a hundred New Zealand mobsters were arrested, and in a subsequent one they targeted dealers in Class A and Class B drugs, and arrested several men known to be career criminals, many of whom were Black Power or Mongrel Mob members.

But as in every other country in the world where organized crime flourishes, for every gangster arrested and jailed, another is ready to step out of the shadows and into his shoes. Organized crime is an endless circle.

Covering an area of around two hundred and seventy thousand square kilometres and with a population of around four million, New Zealand is essentially an agricultural economy. Its capital, Wellington, has a population of around half a million, and Auckland, its major metropolitan area, is home to around a million New Zealanders. With a comparatively small city population, urban street gangs are less of a menace here that they are in other countries. But they do exist, recruiting their members from among young Maoris whose feel themselves disadvantaged by society. It is from these gangs that Black Power, King Cobra, the Nomads and the Mongrel Mob, who between them control the bulk of cannabis cultivation in the country, draw many of their members.

Street gang membership being mainly attractive to Maoris, it is hardly surprising that the tattoos and body markings used to show loyalty to one gang or another and the graffiti used to mark territory are heavily influenced by traditional Maori styles.

At the beginning of *Once Were Warriors*, novelist Alan Duff has one of his central characters pondering Pine Block, the grim council estate on which she lives. Seeing the social deprivation around, she muses, 'Any wonder some ofem [*sic*] wanting to join the gang that'd won the struggle in Pine Block, the Brown Fists. Though there were kids who'd joined their archrivals, the Black Hawks, across town, and so got to do battle, often fatal, with their Pine Block brothers and cousins and childhood friends. Maori against Maori. And thousands ofem each side of the country.'

The book is a novel: but one that says more about New Zealand and its 'street' gangs than academic tomes several times the length.

THE TRIADS

The Triads, China's equivalent of the Mafia, but older by several centuries, are not only involved in organized crime in mainland China and Taiwan, they are the chief producers and distributors of heroin throughout the world and their presence is felt wherever there is a Chinese population.

Before looking at them in some detail, here is a little background information about where they get their heroin from. The Golden Triangle is an area on the borders of Thailand, Burma and Laos and it here that a great deal of the heroin that finds its way onto the world's markets is grown. For decades, probably since the 1960s, the area was controlled by Khun Sa, who directed the flow of heroin from his safe haven in the town of Chiang Mai in northwest Thailand. Surrounded by a mercenary army of local tribesmen and renegade soldiers from the armies of the three countries the

Triangle straddles. He had many allies, but the most important of them all was the CIA!

When the USA withdrew from Vietnam in 1972, the CIA wanted to continue to operate in a covert capacity against the USA's former enemies. The man they turned to was Khun Sa, who was responsible for producing almost all the heroin that was beginning to flood the streets not just of the major cities but of small time America, too.

He gave the Americans a wide-ranging network of routes and sympathetic agents they could use to launch anonymous strikes against Vietnamese-backed forces in Laos. Information that Khun Sa gave the Americans that led them to uncover the existence of hundreds of US

Picking opium, South Vietnam/Thailand.

prisoners still being held in Vietnamese jails.

Khun Sa's role was never officially revealed. How could Washington tell the American people that their main ally in its war against the spread of communism in Southeast Asia was the world's most prolific heroin manufacturer? Today, much of the heroin produced in the Golden Triangle ends up in the hands of Chinese Triads operating in Southeast Asia from where it is smuggled through Turkey into Europe and the United States.

The Triads had been operating in the area for decades. During the early days of America's involvement in Vietnam, the criminal underworld there was ruled by the Binh Xuyen. Based in Saigon, it had been the number one gang in the days when the French ruled Vietnam and in the decade that followed. When the French withdrew and left the Viet Minh in control of the north, the Triad family considered allying itself with the communists, but soon realized that the puppet regime in Saigon, under the nominal rule of the emperor Bao Dai backed by the Americans.

The leader of the Binh Xuyen at this time was Lee Van Vien, also known as Bay Vien, who had been a driver for the French occupation forces in the early 1940s. Before the struggle for power between the communist and the south intensified in the early days of the 1960s, Bay Vien was installed as manager of the Grande Monte, the biggest gambling house in Cholon, the suburb of Saigon that the Chinese had made

their own. From here, Bay Vien started to build up the heroin trade.

He was encouraged in this by Bao Dai, who took a share of the profits and turned a blind eye as Bay began to build up his empire. By the early 1950s, Bay and the Binh Xuyen family controlled a hundred of Saigon's stores, including the city's largest department store, and as many brothels, among then the famous Hall of Mirrors, and a countless number or river boats.

The gangsters were so powerful that when South Vietnam was created as an independent state in 1955 with Ngo Dinh Diem as president, the Binh Xuyen was so determined to re-establish the status quo that gangsters organized a march on the presidential palace. The president retaliated by ordering troops to fire on the Triads. They fled the city, at first to the Rung Sat swamps, but the Ngo Dinh Diem was bent on eradicating them, and ordered his troops to drive them from their stronghold.

Defeated, the Binh Xuyen dispersed, and control of the heroin trade passed to other less organized gangs. Later, with more and more American 'military advisers' pouring into the area, these gangs had a huge new 'home' market for their drugs as well as the traditional export trade.

When the Americans eventually withdrew, it was assumed that the victorious Communists with their intolerance of organized crime would flush these gangs out. They tried, but to no avail. And today, the Vietnamese drug trade is still controlled by gangs such as the Saigon Cowboys and the Young Turks, who follow the traditions of Triad gangs that date back centuries.

A society shrouded in secrecy

The Triad Society began as a secret society in southern China in the late seventeenth century. According to one legend, it came about when the Manchu dynasty decided to rid itself of the troublesome monks in the Songshan Shaolin Temple who had given refuge to rebel troops from Taiwan. Two Manchu officials bribed one of the warrior monks to let them into the monastery via a secret passage and set fire to it. Only five people survived the blaze. They formed themselves into the Hung Family League, and dedicated themselves to overthrowing the Manchu dynasty. The sect established a new monastery in the village of Chuan Chow, and soon started to attract more and more members.

The sect became known by other names, one of which was the Three United or Triad. As the years passed it came to form a sort of covert regional government, looking after the interests of local people against the oppressive central government. Various attempts were made to overthrow the emperor, but each one met with failure. Each time, the survivors fled abroad to escape the revenge of the Manchus, establishing Chinese colonies all over Southeast Asia.

The struggle to remove the government became seemingly more and more hopeless, and more and more

expensive. And so, needing money to fund their political aims, the Triads turned to crime, not just in China, but in the Chinatowns of neighbouring countries. They made money in gambling, prostitution, robbery, kidnappings, extortion and of course from trafficking heroin. Soon the Triads became not the dominant force in the Chinese underworld, it was the Chinese underworld.

At the centre of power

In 1911, General Sun Yat-sen (said to be a member of the Hong Kong Triads) led the revolution that overthrew the imperial dynasty and established a republic. The Triads, knowing that the revolution could not have happened without their help, demanded a seat at the table, and for the next four decades they were firmly at the heart of Chinese government. Membership of a Triad family was more or less necessary for someone who wanted a position in the civil service in Peking. In other cities, free from imperial control, Triad families fought on the streets for control of the lucrative rackets that were now being run openly.

The Nationalist Republic was swept aside in the aftermath of World War Two, when the Communists led by Mao Tse-tung seized control. The defeated government fled to Formosa (Taiwan) with the Triads clinging to their coat tails, where they still flourish to this day.

Included in the many Triad families that are based in Taiwan are the Sung Lio, with several hundred members, mostly second and third generation native-born Taiwanese. Its activities include debt collecting, massage parlours and brothels. The Tian Dao Man family has around the same number of members and is involved identical areas of activities. Bigger than these two families is the Four Seas with up to two thousand members. Its members are active in the construction industry and security services as well as debt collecting, massage parlours and brothels. Biggest of all is probably the United Bamboo family with around ten thousand members. It shares many of its activities with the other families, but adds loan-sharking, gambling dens and hostess clubs to the businesses it runs.

The Triads abroad

In other parts of the world the Triads make a fortune not just from these activities but from the heroin trade. When they need to expand their operations beyond the world's Chinatowns, they often liaise with the Mafia, whose tentacles reach

Gambling joint, Macau. Much gambling in Southeast Asia is run by Triad gangs.

wider into the population. China-towns have grown up in every big city in the world, as the hard-working, entrepreneurial Chinese have emigrated from their native land in search of freedom and the opportunity to make an honest living. And wherever there is a Chinatown there are Triad gangsters, each affiliated to one of a number of rival Triad families. Usually the families come to a mutual under-standing over the territories they run and the activities they control with them. But when no understanding can be reached, 'Triad Wars' break out. There's an outbreak of shootings, knife fights and machete attacks that lasts until the dispute it settled and things get back to normal.

Bloodshed within Chinatowns is sometimes intensified by rivalries between Vietnamese gangs who recruit their members from the large number of Vietnamese refugees who live cheek by jowl with the Chinese in some cities.

In London, Triad gangs used to control most of the massage parlours and run many of the prostitutes in Soho – the city's red light district. But in recent years Albanian and Russian gangs have muscled in on this profitable area of criminal activity. A recent survey, highlighted by the Home Office, suggested that up to seventy per cent of the area's saunas and massage parlours are controlled by Albanian and Kosovan gangs and that the number of Thai and Filipina women being sold into prostitution by Triad gangs has declined. And with Russian, Lithuanian and Polish women replacing oriental prostitutes on the streets of London (often lured to the city by promises of a place to study English), the Triads have moved their prostitutes on to the streets of Manchester, Glasgow and other major cities.

Trafficking in human life

Their income hit by competition from Eastern European gangs, the Triads and another group of gangs, the Snakeheads, have moved into the lucrative illegal immigration business. Snakehead gangs alone are believed to have brought around half a million illegal immigrants into Europe. Native Chinese pay up to £20,000 to be smuggled across international borders to London's Soho and the other Chinatowns all over the continent. The fact that many of the 'native' Chinese have their roots in Hong Kong and the illegal immigrants come from mainland China causes problems of its own. But the gangs who bring the people in care little for that. They are in it for the money. Across Europe the business is thought to yield $8 billion a year.

Many of the illegal immigrants find it impossible to raise the money needed in a lump sum. Always happy to oblige, the Triads and Snakeheads are willing to be paid in instalments from future earnings. If the illegal immigrants fall behind with the payments, not only are they liable to be beaten up, but pressure is put on their families back home to force them to pay up.

Some of the people brought in illegally are put to work in the sweatshop businesses run by the gangs, the instalments being deducted from the meagre wages they are paid.

It's not just the gangs who profit from the trade in illegal immigrants. In Britain, many Chinese have been moved by the gangs who brought them to the country to Norfolk where they are exploited in local food-processing plants, being paid as little as £2 an hour. Work is often provided by 'gangmasters' who employ illegal immigrants on a day-to-day, cash-in-hand, no-questions-asked basis. Unscrupulous landlords cash in on their presence. They rent their houses to illegal immigrants for £40 per person per week. When police broke into a suspect small, three-bedroom house in Norfolk, they found eighteen Chinese workers asleep. That's just less than £3,000 a month for a house that would normally fetch £125 a week on the open market.

Sister Ping

Police in Holland recently scored a notable success against the 'people smugglers' when they arrested Jing Ping Chen, a diminutive Chinese woman who lived in Rotterdam. She is, the authorities claim, responsible for bringing in more than two hundred thousand people into the EU and from there, many of them into the United Kingdom. Sadly, their number is thought to include the fifty-eight Chinese men who suffocated to death in an airtight container when they were being smuggled into the country via Dover.

Better known as 'Sister Peng', Jing Ping Chen was one of the most ruthless figures in the business. Using a combination of violence and intimidation, the slightly built, five-foot-tall Chinese woman swept her rivals aside and cornered the market in people smuggling between Holland and Britain not long after she had arrived in Rotterdam in 1997. Using her connections with the Triads (her boyfriend is the head of the city's 14K gang) she hired the muscle to do her dirty work whenever necessary. One victim was lucky to get off with having his teeth broken when a gun was pushed into his mouth. Another was so badly beaten up that his lungs were punctured.

When a rival mobster tried to muscle in on Sister Peng's territory, she invited him to dinner in Rotterdam's Orient restaurant, a place she often used for meetings, to discuss ways of dividing up the operation between them. But no sooner had he arrived than he was dragged to a room on the first floor, beaten with a hammer and 'kneecapped' – shot in both legs (a favourite method of intimidating enemies used by another gang – the IRA).

According to the police, Sister Ping ran a very smooth operation that cost her around £35,000 a month. She had at least eight people on her payroll, ran a fleet of eight cars as well as other vehicles and owned several safe houses.

Her agents back home in China approached likely migrants and after negotiating a hefty deposit (the balance to be paid from future earnings) they were brought to Europe via a number of routes, controlled all the way along them by Sister Peng's agents. Those who wanted to come to Britain were put in safe houses for a few weeks, waiting for an opportunity to cross to Dover or another suitable south coast port. Once in the country, they were told to claim political asylum or were whisked off to low-paid, unskilled jobs. Sister Ping herself earned around £15 million from her few years in the business.

It was the deaths of those Chinese en route to Dover that led to her downfall. At first, police thought it was a Rotterdam-based Turkish gangster Guersel Ozkham who was the mastermind behind the operation. He was arrested and sentenced to ten years in jail, even though police came to believe that he had been taking orders from above. Ozkham would not talk. But his ex-girlfriend did and pointed the Dutch police in the right direction.

Sister Ping had gone into hiding within hours of the deaths at Dover, but she was tracked down after a massive police operation and sent to trial. She was sentenced to three years in jail for human trafficking and fined £8,000. She was though, cleared of direct involvement in the Dover tragedy.

Had Sister Ping been convicted on drug trafficking on the same scale, she would have received a much heftier sentence. And that's the beauty of people-smuggling to the gangs involved in the trade: less risk of being caught; if you are caught, a less harsh sentence. And huge profits to be made.

Snakehead operations are different

from the Triads in several respects, one being that whereas snakeheads have no formal structure, most Triad families have a well-established and rigid hierarchy. Their officers are ascribed names which, in their original Chinese that hark back to the society's quasi-religious heritage. Translated into sobriquets like Dragon Head, White Paper Fan and Incense Master, they lose much of their mystery. The leader, the *Shan Chu*, has a deputy, *Fu Shan Chu*. Beneath him are the Incense Master (*Heung Chu*) and Vanguard (*Sin Fung*) who at one time were responsible for the religious ceremonies that were once common practice but which are now increasingly a thing of the past.

Pak Tsz Sin (White Paper Fan) is the Triad equivalent of the Mafia *consigliere*. Usually a man of some education, he discusses the strategies and future policies that are put into effect by the *Hung Kwan* (Red Pole). They are the family's enforcers and disciplinarians – and hit men. Once skilled in the marital arts, they are now much more likely to be able to yield a knife with considerable skill and shoot a moving target with lethal accuracy! Red Poles are the men who lead raids on rival Triad families when internecine wars break out (something that happens increasingly often).

The gang member who oversees the activities of the lower ranks, the *Sze Kau*, in their day-to-day criminal activities is the *Chu Chi*. Beneath him there is often a *Dai Lo* who runs the street gangs and sometimes drugs couriers. In London's Chinatown (the area in the square roughly formed by Wardour Street in the west, Charing Cross Road in the east, Shaftesbury Avenue in the north and Coventry Street in the south) Dai Los recruit local, non-Chinese street-wise kids who carry out the really menial tasks on the Triad menu of crime. Equipped with mobile phones and often armed with knives, these lowest-of-the-low in the Triad hierarchy are increasingly a thorn in the flesh of London's already over-stretched police force.

Not being full-time Triads, the kids recruited by a Dai Lo are not required to take part in any initiation ceremony. But in many families, members higher up in the structure are. Based on a ceremony that once took three days to complete but now filleted of most of the ritual and lasting around an hour, initiations are still full of symbolism. In one hangover from the past, in many families recruits must drink from a bowl that contains his own blood mixed with the blood of a cockerel and the ashes of a piece of yellow paper on which his name was written before the paper was set alight. All new members are required to swear thirty-six oaths and to accept that if they fail to adhere to them, they will pay the appropriate price. Death.

FOR LOVE OF A GANGSTER'S MOLL!

IN 1937, King Edward VIII of Great Britain abdicated because he knew that the British people would never accept the woman he loved, Wallis Simpson, as their queen. He was advised by politicians that a morganatic marriage, whereby he could marry Mrs Simpson but that she would never be crowned queen, was out of the question. The problem was not that Mrs Simpson was a gangster's moll (although in her youth she had been a noted poker player in the clubs of Shanghai and probably knew a hood or two) but that she was divorced – twice.

Sixty-six years later, Prince Johan Friso, second son of Queen Beatrix of the Netherlands, could have been forgiven had he looked back and thought, 'Divorce? If only!', for his engagement to a beautiful woman had caused just as big a furore in Holland as the Abdication did in Britain.

Blonde, beautiful and intelligent, Mabel Wisse Smit was, on the face of it, the ideal wife for the Dutch prince. She had worked for the United Nations, was a specialist in Balkan affairs, and since 1997 had been a leading human-rights activist at the Open Society Institute, funded by American billionaire, George Soros.

As is usual in such cases, when the prince made his choice of wife known, she was vetted by the Dutch secret service who declared her a suitable choice. That done, the engagement was made known and the Dutch prime minister, Jan Peter Balkenende, asked for parliament's approval something which was necessary before the couple could get married.

But no sooner had news of the engagement been made public than a former associate of a notorious Dutch gangster, Klaas Bruinsma, claimed that she had been their boss's mistress. She was, according to Charlie da Silva, the only woman who was allowed on Bruinsma's yacht *Neeltje Jacoba*, and the two had been lovers.

Dubbed 'Mabelgate' the Dutch newspapers were soon full of little else.

The claim that Ms Wisse Smit and the gangster, Klaas Bruinsma, had been anything other that acquaintances was strenuously denied. Ms Smit admitted that she had known

Edward and Mrs Simpson meet the Fuhrer.

Bruinsma, known in the underworld as 'the Dutch Godfather', only vaguely through a joint love of sailing. She had spent a night or two on the yacht. But there was no truth at all in the gossip that they had been lovers. It was nonsense. So, too was the claim that she had known that Bruinsma had had two hundred people working for him in drugs and prostitution rackets across Europe and had been linked to several gangland murders before he had himself been murdered in 1991.

As soon as she had found out where his money had come from, she had broken the acquaintanceship.

Prince Friso confirmed that he would carry on with his request for parliament's approval. The prime minister, bowing to pressure from the Dutch Socialist Party, said that, in view of the claim, there would have to be an official inquiry.

Within days Balkenende told a press conference that he was unable to give his support to the marriage. He said that Ms Wisse Smit had given 'false and incomplete information' and that 'trust had been violated'.

As details continued to emerge, Ms Wisse Smit admitted that she had spent several nights on Bruinsma's yacht over an eighteen month period. But she continued to deny that there had been any sexual relationship.

The couple apologized to Queen Beatrix. In a published letter they said that they had decided 'not to conceal her [Ms Wisse Smit's] contacts with Bruinsma, but to give as many details as possible. We were hoping to prevent what has now happened: the recall of painful memories that Mabel had hoped were long past.' The letter went on to say that the couple realized that they had been 'naïve' and 'unwise'.

But Prince Friso reiterated his intention to go ahead with the marriage. To do so, he renounced his claim to the throne.

Perhaps it is unfair to dub Mabel Wisse Smit as a gangster's moll. But there is no denying that Klass Bruinsma was a particularly unsavoury character. Born into a wealthy brewing family, he became increasingly involved in drug dealing and prostitution and came to dominate the Dutch underworld. But his supremacy started to unravel after forty-five tonnes of cannabis with a street value of £150 million were seized by the police. Not long afterwards, he was shot in the early hours of the morning after a drinking session in the Amsterdam Hilton had ended a violent argument.

He had been a notoriously violent criminal. One of his rivals had been found upside down in a barrel of cement having had his legs and penis cut off. A post mortem showed that the limbs and sexual organ had been severed while the unfortunate victim was still alive!

GANG SLANG

Everyone knows a gangster's moll is the broad on his arm, that a 'brief' is a criminal's lawyer (usually one who, when he claims in court that his client is not guilty, should do so with his (or her) fingers crossed behind his (or her) back), and that Jewish Lightning is a fire that has been started deliberately for insurance purposes: hence the expression that behind every successful self-made businessman there's two bankruptcies and a bit of Jewish Lightning. But what about 'Kibbles and Bits' and a 'Luther'? Both are included in this all-too-brief explanation of some of the expressions of the words that gangsters and other underworld characters use when they are talking to each other.

Accelerator	An arsonist and the fuel that is used to start a fire
Across the Pavement	A wages snatch
Air Dance	An execution by hanging
Alkali Alki	Bootleg booze
American Way	An arrangement between rival gangs and Mafia to co-exist peacefully
Apache Indian Job	A fire bomb that does its job so well that there is nothing left behind. Often used in a piece of Jewish Lighting
Archer	UK gang slang for two grand – the amount Lord Archer is alleged to have given the prostitute to whose services he is alleged to have taken recourse to buy her silence
Arm	The faction of the Cosa Nostra based in Buffalo, New York
Arm Candy	A moll who prefers older men, usually seen in expensive restaurants to boost his ego She may or may not be expected to reward her men with sexual services – if he is up for it
Ashes, Hauling one's	Having sex with a prostitute or casual pick-up
Banana	US gang slang for heroin that is being trafficked
Babbler	Australian rhyming slang for a criminal (babbling brook = crook)
Back Gate Discharge	American for a prisoner on Death Row who is taken out the back door to the execution cell so that his fellow prisoners will not be upset
Bad	Better than good
Bad rap	A prison sentence of more than twenty years
Baggage	A non-participant spectator at a card game
Bale	In the US, a pound of marijuana
Banana Race	A horse race, the result of which has been fixed
Bangkok Connection	The route via which drugs are taken from Southeast Asia via Bangkok to North America (Dangerous because of the harsh sentences handed out for drug trafficking in Thailand: ask Sandra Gregory!)

Barbecue Stool	The electric chair
Beauty Doctor	A club tipped with steel used to ensure that the victim of a beating-up will be permanently disfigured
B-Girl	A girl who works in an American brothel where drinks are sold
Big Gates	An American penitentiary
Big Papa	The Thompson machine gun widely used in Chicago during the Prohibition gang wars
Bino	A riot in an American prison
Blanket Party	The practice in US jails by which a blanket is thrown over the imminent victim of a beating-up or gang rape, to avoid identification
Blind Pig	A Prohibition expression for an illicit drinking den
Blow Away	To kill someone by shooting
Boilermaker	A conman who specializes in parting middle-aged women from their money
Books	In Mafia parlance, books are open when there is a vacancy that needs to be filled, and closed when there is no need to recruit new members
The Boss of Bosses	The Numero Uno – the capo de tutti capi – the undisputed leader of the US Mafia
Bower Bird	Australian slang for a petty thief
Boxcar	A prison cell
Brass Eye	A prison cell that can only be locked and unlocked electronically
Brief	A lawyer
Brown Eye	A sawn-off shotgun
Bug	US gang slang for a criminal who is one hundred per cent lacking in feeling
Bullet	A one year-sentence in a US jail
Bumbles	Ecstasy (rhyming slang Bumble bee = ecstasy)
Burning coal	A US prison term describing a sexual relationship between a black and white inmate
Bus therapy	The practice of moving American prisoners from one penitentiary to another to keep them away from criminal contacts on the outside
Buttonhole	US prison slang for recruiting a new member to a gang of inmates
Caballo	Someone who smuggles drugs into prison (From the Spanish for 'horse')
Cadillac	An ounce of heroin in a US jail
Cafone	A US phoney who is just as embarrassed by his own behaviour as others are on his behalf
Calling card	A fingerprint
Canary	A police informer
Cap	Either drugs in capsule form or oral sex
Capodecima	A gang member who controls a gang of ten junior gangsters
Case dough	A nest egg acquired from the proceeds of crime, theoretically untouchable
Catch a stack	To rob someone of a large amount of money
Catch out	To ask for prospective custody in a US prison
Catfish death	In the US a suicide by drowning
Cat house	A brothel
Cat-up	An American armed robbery
Cement overcoat	A way of killing someone by smearing his body with concrete and then when it is hardened, throwing the victim, still alive, into water. Also known as a cement coffin or cement shoes

Chairman of the Board	The highest-ranking member of a Cosa Nostra Family
Chapper	A policeman
Charlie	Usually cocaine, but in Australia a hooker
Chased	To be driven from a Mafia family and forbidden to do business with them
Chase the Dragon	To burn heroin on foil and sniff the fumes or inhale them through a tube. Safer than injecting in these days of AIDS-infected needles
Cherries	Greyhounds (Rhyming slang: cherry hogs = dogs)
Chicago leprosy	Sores caused by the use of hypodermic needles
Chicago piano	The Thompson machine gun popular with Chicago gangsters during Prohibition
Chief corrupter	The Family member responsible for bribing politicians
Chiv	A knife, cut-throat razor or any other sharp weapon used to attack a victim. Also a verb, meaning to attack someone with such a weapon
Choirboy	A newly recruited police officer
Choir practice	An after-duty meeting attended by US policemen for drink and sex
Cholo	A member of the same gang
Clean skin	Not having a criminal record (Australian)
Cockatoo	The lookout at an illegal Australian gambling school
Cold Storage	Solitary confinement in an American jail
College	A British borstal or an American state penitentiary
Comare	A gangster's girlfriend
Come heavy	Come armed with a loaded gun
Comp	A female employee in a US casino who is told by the management to offer sexual services to high-playing customers
Concaves	In Australia, a pack of fixed playing cards
Contract	An arranged killing
Connection	The relationship between an inferior criminal and a superior one who will protect him from others and the police in return for services rendered
Cop a knocker	To be arrested
Cop and blow	To pimp for a temporary prostitute, making her work long hours over a short period of time
Coppertime	Remission from a prison sentence
Corner game	A scam whereby stolen goods are offloaded to someone who is then arrested by men posing as police officers who make it known that they can be bribed with cash and the stolen goods
Coyote	Someone who transports illegal immigrants across the Mexican border into the US
Creeping and tilling	Stealing from shop tills in the US
Crew	Mafia men under the command of a street captain
Croak	To die
Cugine	A man about to be initiated into the Mafia
Cut off at the knees	To be in the position of having no remedy or options
Dab	A fingerprint
Dance floor	The condemned cell
Datastreaming	Credit card fraud whereby details of a card are hacked in a retail store and used to create counterfeit cards that are usually sold for use abroad
Deadbeat	Someone who borrows money but has no intention of settling the debt

Dead pigeon	Someone who is accused of a crime, the evidence against whom is undeniable
Deep six	To kill someone: from the old navy habit of dropping unwanted items overboard to sink six fathoms deep
Dibble	A policeman: from the hapless cop who tried to pit his wits against *Top Cat*
Dirty	Being caught in possession of drugs or illegal weapons
Disneyland	A prison with a reputation for treating inmates well
District Man	A member of a gang who controls crime in a small urban area
Dixie cup	A hired hitman who will be killed once the contract has been fulfilled
Dog food	A mainly American term for heroin
Do the business	To fulfil a contract
Drive-by	A random shooting from a passing car
Dutch act	Suicide
Dynamite	Any drug that is more potent that usual
Eagle	An American criminal who works alone
Elbow	An American policeman
Eliminate	To kill
Empty Suit	A would-be gang member who has nothing to offer the gang he wished to join
Equalize	To kill someone
Erase	To equalize
Eye	A detective
Eye wash	In the US, tear gas
Fag hag	A woman who seeks out the company of homosexual men
Fall guy	Someone who is set up to take responsibility for a crime of which he is innocent
Fat	In the US, to be well supplied with drugs
Fat man	The electric chair
Fibbies	The FBI
Finger	To name names to the police
Fireproofer	An American conman who preys on religious fanatics
Firm	A gang (UK)
Fit up	To plant evidence on someone to ensure conviction
Flap man	An Australian who bounces bad cheques
Flea	An inmate in an Australian prison who manages to be on good terms with his fellow inmates and with the warders
Flop	The time between two meetings of the parole board in the US
Flying lesson	When someone throws himself or someone else off a prison landing, he is said to have taken such instruction
Foot soldier	The lowest of the low in a criminal organization
Form	A police record
Freehander	A particularly good forger in the US
Frog	A girl who will hop into bed with anyone
Fruitfly	A fag hag by any other name
Fugazi	Counterfeit money
Gaffle up	To arrest a gang member in the US
Gage	In the US, a shotgun
Gangbanger	A member of a street gang on the West Coast of the US

Garter	A prison sentence that may be lengthened or shortened at the discretion of the court
Gas	To get into an elderly person's house by pretending to be from the Gas Board, which although bad is preferable to its US meaning, which is to throw fluid at a prison guard
Gatemouth	Someone who talks too much for their own good
Get a place ready	To prepare an inconspicuous grave for the victim of a contract
Get the big picture	To be the victim of a contract
Ghetto star	A criminal, usually a drug dealer, who has achieved celebrity status in his own neighbourhood
Gin-mill	A US bar
Gladiator school	A prison where particularly troublesome young criminals do their time
Goat throttling	A method used by the Mafia to kill their enemies. A noose is put round the victim's neck and a single cord passed through it, attached to the hands and feet; the more the victim struggles, the tighter the noose becomes
Go on the line	In the US, to join a gang
Goner	A person on whom a contract has been taken out or successfully fulfilled
Gopher	A safe with a hard-to-crack time lock
Got a permanent wave	Died on the electric chair
Goulash	In the US, misleading information
Grass	An informer: to inform
Gray	A US term for a white Caucasian male
Green goods game	A con trick which leaves the victim holding a wad of newspaper rather than the bank notes he believes it to be
Grub	In New Zealand, a term for information
Gullion	Stolen gems
Gypsy cab	In New York, an unlicensed taxi
Half-assed wiseguy	A man who wished to be admitted to a Mafia family
Ham and cheese sandwich	The pay-off received by an American union delegate in a rigged election
Hang it on the limb	To escape from an American prison
Hardware	Weapons, usually firearms
Harlem sunset	A knife wound that proves to be fatal
Head	The victim of a crime in the US
Headhunter	A contract killer
Heavy work	An armed robbery
Hen pen	A female prison
High siding	Showing off
Hobbit	A prisoner who knuckles down and does his time, playing it by the rule and causing no trouble
Homey	A member of the same neighbourhood gang
Hoosegow	A US prison
Horse to horse	All things being equal
Hot wire	To start a car by short-circuiting the ignition wires
Hustler	Either a confidence trickster or a male prostitute
Icebox	The solitary confinement prison cell
Illywhacker	A small-time confidence trickster who plays the country fair circuit
In back	The condemned cell

Ink	A US tattoo
In the hat	Someone who is said to be 'in the hat' has been marked for death
In the mix	Being a member of a gang
Italian football	A bomb
Italian necktie	A two-man way of killing a victim by wrapping a length of rope around his neck, both killers then pulling at an end each
Jacket	The file the US police holds on a known criminal
Jack Mack	In the US, a tin of sardines or other fish put in a sock and used as a cosh
Jam a Pete	In the US, to fail to open the combination lock on a safe because the tumblers have been lined up wrongly
Jargoon	A worthless diamond-like stone passed of as the real thing by a conman
Jeans at half mast	To be caught at something of a disadvantage
Jennybarn	A low-class US brothel, often little more than the back room of a bar
Jigaboo	A US term for an Afro-American
Jive	Lies
Job	A criminal act
Joe	A firearm in the US
Joeying	Specializing in theft from handbags
Jolly beans	Benzedrine
Jolt	In the US, either to sentence to imprisonment or to die in the electric chair
Jump in	To be initiated into a US gang
Jump up	To steal from the back of a parked truck by jumping into the back and handing stuff down to an accomplice
Junk tank	In the US, a prison cell in which an alcoholic or drug addict is held
K	A large stash of drugs
Kamikaze move	A prison killing carried out in full view of a warder
Keester bunny	A US term for someone who pushes contraband in his rectum to get it past Customs
Kickback	A bribe, usually to a policeman or other official, often a percentage of the profit of a crime
Kick off	A US term for dying
Knife	American verb for swindling
Kibbles and bits	Cocaine crumbs
King bung	An American brothel keeper
Kiss of death	The kiss given on the cheek to the intended victim of a Mafia assassination
Kitty kitty	An American prison wardress
Kneecap	To shoot someone in the knee or drill a hole in it. Widely used by the IRA after the Bloody Sunday shootings both as a punishment and a warning to others to toe the line
Knockings	The closing pleas in a criminal trial when both lawyers attempt to knock the opposing side's arguments
Knock up	To steal
Kokomo	An American cocaine addict
Lagger	An Australian police informer
Latest Thing on the Beach	A young man, just arrived in jail, weighed up for his sexual attraction to other inmates

Laughing academy	A US term for mental asylum
Lay paper	To pass dud cheques
Lead poisoning	Gunshot wounds in the US
Leg hanger	An American prisoner who fraternizes with the wardens
Lettuce	A US term for paper money
Line-up	An identification parade
Liquidate	To kill someone
Loan shark	Someone who lends money illegally, usually at exorbitant rates
Long rod	A rifle or shotgun
Looking like rain	An arrest is imminent
Lush roller	A pickpocket (dip) who practises his trade on drunks
Luther	A visit to a prisoner
Made man	Someone who has been inducted into a Mafia family
Make	To induce someone into the Mafia, after which he is a made man
Marble orchard	A graveyard attached to an American prison
Meat eater	A policeman who is known to be open to accepting bribes
Mechanic	A hired assassin
Ming	The police
Miss Emma	Morphine
Moggies	Amphetamines
Money	A US term for best friend
Mouse	An American police informer
Mug shot	A police photograph
Mule	Someone who carries drugs across national borders for a tiny fraction of their street value
Moustache Pete	A member of the Mafia in the first decades of the last century, either born in Sicily or first generation of Sicilian parents
Nark	A police informer
Necktie	The hangman's noose
Nevada gas	A US term of cyanide
Ninja	The HIV virus
Nod the Nut	An Australian term for admitting guilt
Nose candy	Cocaine
Notice	A contract given to a hit man
Nuts	Expenses incurred in setting up a theft
Old Smokey	The electric chair, also known as 'Old Sparkey', especially in Florida
On the game	Being involved in prostitution
On the one	To be honest
On the plastic	Using stolen credit and debit cards for fraudulent purposes
Out to lunch	In the wrong
Ox	A razorblade used in a slashing
Pack rat	An insignificant thief
Padding	When police add to the quantity of drugs seized in a bust to make the arrest more significant than it is, they are said to have been padding it
Palm oil	A bribe
Pastel	An American term for an unmarked police car
Patches	Bright yellow patches sewn on to the uniforms of prisoners who are thought to be likely escapees
Peach	To inform
Pen	A US term for prison

People	An American term for the close friends of family of a prisoner
Piece of the business	A share of the proceeds of a crime: also known as a piece of the action
Pineapple	A bomb
Piss it out the window	To squander the proceeds of a crime on wine, women and song
Pocket man	The gang member who is entrusted with the proceeds of a crime before they are shared between the others involved
Pollo	An illegal Mexican immigrant to the USA
Poogie	A US term for prison
Puppies	Shoes
Put down	To be sent to jail
Put on armour	To stuff newspapers under prison clothes to protect against being stabbed during a fight in a US prison
Take a powder	To run away from the scene of a crime
Queer quartet	The four guards who take in turn to watch in pairs over a condemned man waiting in the death cell
Rabbi	An experienced police officer who is the mentor of a junior officer in the early stages of his career
Rabbit blood	A US term for a strong desire to escape from prison
Rank	To double cross
Rapper	A US term for the person pressing charges against an accused man
Rats	Dice
Red penny man	An Australian term for a pimp
Ride on	A shooting from a passing car
Right arm	The second-in-command in a Mafia family. Also known as Under boss
Road dog	An American term for a close friend
Rockafella	US gang slang for killing someone
Rod	A gun (usually a hand pistol)
Rolled up	To be arrested
Sail	To be released on bail from a US jail
San Quentin Quail	A US term for a sexually attractive girl who is obviously under the age of consent; AKA jailbait
Satellite	A US way of describing someone who hangs around a gang hoping to be accepted into it
Scrum down	A meeting of Australian policemen held to ensure that their stories will dovetail during an upcoming trial
Serious headache	A bullet wound in the head
Set trip	To change gangs
Shank	A sharp weapon, usually but not necessarily a knife
Sheet	In the United States, having form
Shooting gallery	A place where drug addicts get together to take drugs, usually by injection
Shyster	A crooked brief
Sicilian necktie	A wire garrotte
Skid artist	The driver of a getaway car
Sky pilot	A prison priest
Slammer	Prison
Sleep	A prison sentence (three years in the UK, one in the US)
Smogged	Executed in the gas chamber
Snide shooter	A false firearm
Soldier	The lowest-ranking member of a Mafia family

Sort out	To influence a witness's testimony, usually by bribery or intimidation
Speedball	An injection of cocaine and heroin
Spondulicks	Money
Squat seat	The electric chair
Squeal	To inform
Stand-up man	A gangster who will never inform on fellow gang members even if offered a deal by the police for doing so
Stew	An Australian term for a fixed sporting event, usually a horse race
Stiff	A dead body
Sting	A confidence trick
Strapped	Carrying a gun
Suke	Mafya slang for an informer
Sweetener	A bribe
Swing	To die by hanging
Swordsman	Someone who receives stolen goods
22-50 nark	An American grass
Tailgate	To drive bumper to bumper to the car in front
Take a fall	To be arrested or put down
Talk cabbage	Frank talking and cooperation between officers of different police forces
Tap city	Broke
Throwdown	A firearm planted by US police at the scene of a shooting to suggest that the unarmed victim of a police shooting was armed
Thumper	A US term for a firearm
Time	A prison sentence
Tooting a line	Sniffing cocaine
Traps	Australian police
Trunk music	The noise made by the decaying flesh of a corpse locked in the boot of a car after a US gangland killing
Tunnel	To defraud or swindle
Two's up	Sharing
Uncle Sugar	The FBI
Under glass	Being in prison
Vega	A marijuana cigar
Viper mad	Addicted to marijuana
Wannabe	A youngster who wants to be a member of a gang
Warehouse	Prison
Wedge	A wad of banknotes
Wide	Cunning or experienced
Wilas	A letter smuggled out of prison by the member of a gang asking for something to be done by a fellow member
Word Up	American for the truth
X	Ten dollars
Yale	Crack cocaine
Yardbird	The inmate of a US jail
Yoke	A US term for cutting someone's throat from behind

Extracted with kind permission from *Gang Slang* by James Morton
Published 2002 by Virgin Books, London